About This Book

Why is this topic important?

Video is everywhere. Your friends shoot video on their smart phones and send it to you to illustrate something important in their lives. You send your students to a YouTube or TeacherTube link to see a demonstration.

The video might be a little wobbly or the sound isn't as good as you'd like or it doesn't show exactly what you want, but you use it because it's available.

This book will help you create video that suits your purpose exactly and looks professional. Your students understand that the content in the video is important because the video looks like what they expect video to look like. It communicates well, at the explicit level of the content and the implicit level of the production quality.

But you didn't hire video producers to make the video. You used this book, inexpensive equipment, and the professional techniques described here to make video that works for you and your students.

Whether you're a teacher, corporate trainer, librarian, or even someone who does have the funding and needs to hire professionals, this book will help you produce the video you need and make it available to your learners.

What can you achieve with this book?

You can create videos to use in your teaching that are designed for learning and look professional, using inexpensive equipment. You may already have some of the equipment you need, and you may be able to borrow what you don't have.

The keys are planning and using professional techniques. Plan the video to make your shooting time as efficient as possible. Shoot it so you show what is important. Edit it to maintain the learners' interest and direct attention to what is essential. Then distribute it to your learners.

Your video will be useful because it uses the learners' time well and provides access to content that is otherwise hard to see or difficult to get to. Most important, it will fit your ways of teaching and your students' ways of learning because you made it.

How is this book organized?

This book is in five sections. Each section concludes with an assignment.

Section I focuses on planning the video. Chapter 1 offers a rationale for using video now, including reasonable costs for very good equipment and software and the ease with which a teacher or trainer can now produce good video. Chapters 2 through 6 cover different aspects of planning, including scripting and managing video projects.

Section II describes the equipment you will need, including camcorders, lights, and microphones. It also includes a chapter on using the camera. Section III leads you through the pre-production steps, including selecting locations, breaking down the script, and planning the actual shoot, to the actual day of the shoot. Section IV is post-production, including editing, sound, and visual effects. The concluding Section V discusses distribution of the video on discs or the web. The final chapter includes tips on using video in your teaching.

The website (http://cv4tt.tspannaus.com) includes valuable extra material, including teaching guides, sample videos, and material too new to be included in the book. Instructions for registering may be found in the Introduction to this book.

About Pfeiffer

Pfeiffer serves the professional development and hands-on resource needs of training and human resource practitioners and gives them products to do their jobs better. We deliver proven ideas and solutions from experts in HR development and HR management, and we offer effective and customizable tools to improve workplace performance. From novice to seasoned professional, Pfeiffer is the source you can trust to make yourself and your organization more successful.

Essential Knowledge Pfeiffer produces insightful, practical, and comprehensive materials on topics that matter the most to training and HR professionals. Our Essential Knowledge resources translate the expertise of seasoned professionals into practical, how-to guidance on critical workplace issues and problems. These resources are supported by case studies, worksheets, and job aids and are frequently supplemented with CD-ROMs, websites, and other means of making the content easier to read, understand, and use.

Essential Tools Pfeiffer's Essential Tools resources save time and expense by offering proven, ready-to-use materials—including exercises, activities, games, instruments, and assessments—for use during a training or team-learning event. These resources are frequently offered in looseleaf or CD-ROM format to facilitate copying and customization of the material.

Pfeiffer also recognizes the remarkable power of new technologies in expanding the reach and effectiveness of training. While e-hype has often created whizbang solutions in search of a problem, we are dedicated to bringing convenience and enhancements to proven training solutions. All our e-tools comply with rigorous functionality standards. The most appropriate technology wrapped around essential content yields the perfect solution for today's on-the-go trainers and human resource professionals.

Pfeiffer
www.pfeiffer.com

Essential resources for training and HR professionals

Pfeiffer

CREATING VIDEO FOR TEACHERS AND TRAINERS

Producing Professional Video with Amateur Equipment

TIMOTHY W. SPANNAUS

Pfeiffer
A Wiley Imprint
www.pfeiffer.com

Published by Pfeiffer
An Imprint of Wiley
One Montgomery Street, Suite 1200, San Francisco, CA 94104-4594
www.pfeiffer.com

For additional copies/bulk purchases of this book in the U.S. please contact 800-274-4434.

Pfeiffer books and products are available through most bookstores. To contact Pfeiffer directly call our Customer Care Department within the U.S. at 800-274-4434, outside the U.S. at 317-572-3985, fax 317-572-4002, or visit www.pfeiffer.com.

Pfeiffer publishes in a variety of print and electronic formats and by print-on-demand. Some material included with standard print versions of this book may not be included in e-books or in print-on-demand. If this book refers to media such as a CD, DVD, or flash drive that is not included in the version you purchased, you may download this material at http://booksupport.wiley.com. For more information about Wiley products, visit www.wiley.com.

Library of Congress Cataloging-in-Publication Data

Spannaus, Timothy W. (Timothy Wise)
  Creating video for teachers and trainers : producing professional video with amateur equipment /
Timothy W. Spannaus.
    p. cm.
  Includes bibliographical references and index.
  ISBN 978-1-118-08809-8 (pbk.); ISBN 978-1-118-22345-1 (ebk.); ISBN 978-1-118-23675-8 (ebk.);
ISBN 978-1-118-26171-2 (ebk.)
  1. Video tapes in education. 2. Video recordings—Production and direction. 3. Digital media.
4. Education—Audio-visual aids. I. Title.
  LB1044.75.S73 2012
  371.33′5—dc23

                                                                                2012003577

Acquiring Editor: Matthew Davis
Editorial Assistant: Michael Zelenko
Director of Development: Kathleen Dolan Davies
Developmental Editor: Susan Rachmeler
Production Editor: Michael Kay
Editor: Rebecca Taff
Manufacturing Supervisor: Becky Morgan
Author photo: Mary Jane Murawka

Printed in the United States of America
PB Printing   10 9 8 7 6 5 4 3 2 1

For Collette, my leading lady.

CONTENTS

SECTION III: PRODUCTION   113

ACKNOWLEDGMENTS

My students in the Wayne State Instructional Technology program are at the center of this book. They inspired it. They read drafts and improved it. They encouraged me to get it written and off to the publisher. I wrote it for them and their successors.

One group of them stands out, the Fall 2011 Advanced Multimedia class. They critiqued the chapters and used the near-final draft as their text. They made videos as samples, used the sample script, modeled for photos, and pointed me in the right direction to make this book useful for their fellow students and practitioners. They are Wadeeah Alshawi, Charles Barger, Julie Belanger, Alexis Graham, Alfie Green, Fouad Kazma, John Kotarski, and Richard Lerman. I thank them for their contributions to this book. You will see their pictures and feel their influence throughout the book.

Two very creative people did most of the illustrations. Julie Howells and Jeremy Radke made my ideas for illustrations into artwork that communicates the ideas in this very visual medium.

My contacts at Pfeiffer, Matt Davis, Michael Zelenko, and Michael Kay, have made this a much better book with their work to turn a manuscript into something we can all be proud of.

However this book helps you, the reader, to make better video, these people have helped you. If there are any remaining errors or words that are hard to understand, those are my work and I ask your understanding.

Thank you.

INTRODUCTION

The purpose of this book is to help teachers and trainers produce professional quality training videos, using less than professional quality equipment and software.

I am the first to argue that professional results require professionals. So when it really counts, I call on professionals to do the video with their professional gear and studios. But it doesn't always count enough to engage the pros, or maybe I need it quickly, or there is just no budget. Then we use our less expensive consumer-grade gear, but we still approach the task professionally. This is no grab-and-shoot, then play the whole unedited video for a class or put it up on a video sharing site on the web. This is planned, scripted, rehearsed, shot, and edited video, executed with care and forethought. We'll see how to do this in this book. We'll also touch on some of the many ways to put video on the web, DVDs, or other ways of distributing your final product.

We'll go through the process in the book and the accompanying website. More than technique, I'll discuss why you do things the way you do, bringing in research on how people learn from multimedia, how people view video, and the grammar of moving images and sound.

The first section of the book walks through the whole process, in brief, so you know where you're going before you get there. In particular, we'll talk about planning your video.

Then we go on to scripting and storyboarding, basic planning tools to help you think through the video you are going to produce. Of course, things change while you're shooting and editing, but without a plan, you won't even know they've changed.

The next section of the book talks about equipment basics, including selecting a camcorder, using lights to improve the image, and mics to improve the sound. This section includes a practice assignment, just using those tools, to create a short unedited video. You will need to become familiar with these basic tools and learn to use them.

Then we go into detail on the actual shoot. Most often, you'll be "on location," our jargon that means you're not renting a studio. You're in your home or office, on the street, in a classroom, or in a lab. You need to understand the limitations and advantages of location shoots, as well as how to plan for the shoot, making it as trouble-free as possible.

On the shoot, you'll walk through the scenes with your cast, so they know what to do before you shoot. We'll discuss how to make your work as efficient as possible, minimizing scene changes and re-lighting. And you'll see how to track your work, so when you get to edit, you know where each scene is.

Post-production is the phase after you shoot. Review all your video assets, see what you want to use and what, figuratively, hits the cutting room floor. Assemble the scenes you want to use, edit for pace, clarity, and interest, add sounds and effects, and render the video. It may not yet be in the format you want to use, so we'll look at options for making your video available to your students.

But, I can hear you asking, you said we'd talk about learning from multimedia and the grammar of video and the "why" of producing video. Where is that? I've integrated those discussions along with the how-to. The best time to learn why you do something is when you're learning the something itself. Your learning about video will be integrated knowledge, not isolated facts and concepts. Sometimes there will be a sidebar that draws in some cognitive psychology or media literacy. Occasionally, it will be in the text itself, but usually it works better to discuss these ideas by themselves, but in the context of your new skill and knowledge.

Because a book has some serious limitations when it comes to learning to shoot video, there is the website. Many chapters have a counterpart section on the web, with demonstrations of technique and the resulting video.

You may join the website at http://cv4tt.tspannaus.com. Click on Login and follow the directions for "Is this your first time here?" Complete the login process and register for the Creating Video course. When prompted for an enrollment key for the course, enter TimSentMe. Include the period at the end. It is case-sensitive.

Some excellent, patient, knowledgeable video professionals and a lot of my students have helped enormously with the book and site. Enjoy their work and learn from it.

One more comment: You will never watch a movie, TV show, or even home video the same way again. Again and again, students have commented on their changed perception of video and film. Their new knowledge of how things are done brings new enjoyment to watching video. They look at lighting, editing, staging, and blocking with new eyes, sometimes thinking of different or better ways to do a scene.

Happy shooting! And happy viewing.

PLANNING AND MANAGING VIDEO PROJECTS

CHAPTER

1

WHY VIDEO? WHY NOW?

As a teacher or trainer, it might be easy to continue doing things the way we always have. Create a text-heavy PowerPoint, e-learning module, or other instructional media. Those things are easy, we're used to them, and they work the way we think. Written notes have been a mainstay of teaching for millennia. The reformatting of our notes to slides or web pages isn't challenging, we can do it quickly, and our audiences are mostly used to it.

Or are they? Video is everywhere. You can shoot video with your phone or digital camera and load it to YouTube or TeacherTube in minutes. Our learners do it, and they find text used as the principle teaching medium pretty boring, a step backwards.

We also know that our learners, of whatever age, will learn more by using multiple media. Use text with images or text with video, and they will learn more (Mayer, 2009). The research is pretty compelling. And note that we're not using video or images just to keep the learner's attention. The video must contribute to learning; otherwise it's a distraction and can actually inhibit learning (Mayer, 2009).

Selection of video may depend on the content to be learned. Really, some things can be adequately described in text. Philosophy is basically a textual subject, as are many theory courses. And some things require images, sound and others, video. Images work well for geology or geometry. Video is really important for some more topics. Let's look at those.

Our use of video can support learning in many ways. Here's a short list, by no means inclusive:

- Demonstration of a procedure
- A presentation by a noted expert
- Introduction to a case study
- Excerpt of a dramatic production
- Demonstration of a process
- Virtual tours

Let's look at each of these to see how video can help you with teaching and learning.

DEMONSTRATION OF PROCEDURES

Often in education and training we're showing our students how to do something. It might be a physical procedure such as cooking, or a lab procedure in chemistry or biology, or a soft skills procedure like counseling or a performance review.

For some reason many students in my video classes do videos on cooking. Whatever it is, they work. My church has volunteers who bake bread for every service. The quality of the bread was very inconsistent. I made a short video on baking bread and put it up on the website. The quality of the bread has improved. A basic demonstration of a procedure can have a good payoff.

PRESENTATION BY AN EXPERT

For many years in one of my classes I used a video recording of David Merrill explaining, in about twelve minutes, his First Principles paper. It's wonderful. I can explain First Principles in class, but it's better from the author. Dave's a delightful presenter and the use of a video with him shatters the image some students have of well-known researchers as someone distant and impersonal. And they get First Principles. They learn it. No one, after viewing the video, misses the First Principles questions on the midterm.

INTRODUCTION TO A CASE STUDY

There are many uses of case studies in instruction. The website for this book includes one made for a finance company. We're introduced to two characters, Michael and Lisa, who meet each other for the first time in the company cafeteria. The video script leads us into some assumptions about them, then takes an unexpected twist to demonstrate that what we think we know about people is not always true.

The dialog between Michael and Lisa on the website carries an emotional punch that requires the intimacy and story development of video. It would really be hard to make the same point any other way. The module follows up with questions and discussion points about the dialog. The production for the Michael and Lisa video is very high-quality and very expensive. The point is the effectiveness of the script, which was written by a personnel consultant (my brother Fred, actually), not a professional scriptwriter. This kind of script is within the reach of teachers and trainers.

In another low-budget project, a student created a case study video on classroom management. The video sets up the problem and allows the student to choose what to say, taking the role of the teacher. Then the student sees the results of the decision. This project was done by a teacher. The video is integrated into a website, so the posing of choices and branching to see consequences is done with inexpensive technology. This is the kind of low-budget, high impact production that is within your reach. This kind of project is what Aldrich (2005) calls a branching story, a simple but effective simulation.

EXCERPT OF A DRAMATIC PRODUCTION

The laws on DVD excerpts have changed—use a piece from a movie (Network News single camera shoot) or *To Kill a Mockingbird* on civil rights or John Adams on colonial/constitutional period history. Teachers and professors in non-profit institutions have certain rights to use excerpts that trainers or others in for-profits do not. Both should check with their organization's copyright experts.

SHOW A PROCESS

I'll differentiate here between a process and a procedure, following Clark (2008). Procedures may be performed by one person, whereas processes may require many people, or may be highly automated, requiring only human observation and monitoring. Changing a tire, calculating a square root, or baking muffins are procedures. Generating power in a nuclear plant is a process. Assembling an auto is a process. Developing a new academic program or even hiring a new staff member is a process.

Some processes are very difficult to observe. Video can help the learner see things that are not clearly visible, since it might be possible to place a camera and cinematographer in places or circumstances where you might not want to take hundreds of new hire trainees.

The manufacturing process for glass bottles is one such hard-to-observe process. At one end, high above the factory floor, is an oven that heats silica sand, some chemicals, and recycled glass to melting. The molten glass flows through a highly automated machine with many operating parts to one of a dozen or more molds, where the bottle is formed, then deposited on a belt that moves it past an inspection station. Defective bottles are ejected by a blast of compressed air. Good bottles move onto a tempering and cooling area and are then packaged.

There is no place a trainee could stand to see all of this. But we can shoot video from many different places that can be edited together to demonstrate the process from beginning to end.

Oh yes, the environment is noisy and crowded with machinery. The video orients new engineers and technicians to the process from the comfort of the desktop. Yes, they need to get into the plant, but when they get there, they will understand what they're looking at.

VIRTUAL TOURS

A teacher has planned a field trip to the Museum of Science and Industry in Chicago. This is a wonderful museum, with many engaging exhibits. On a visit there, a guard told me that if I looked at each exhibit for thirty seconds, it would take me a month to see the whole museum. And by the time I was finished, the museum would have changed enough that I would need to start over. Whether his calculations are correct or not, there's a lot to see, so much that a visit can be overwhelming for schoolchildren.

A teacher could prepare students for a visit by shooting a virtual tour. An overview of the sections of the museum could be followed by vignettes of interesting sections, like the cafeteria for lunch (let's cover the important things first), the U-boat for students studying World War II, or the coal mine for those studying energy and ecology, or technology exhibits . . . well, you get the picture.

Arranging to shoot video of a museum for a virtual tour will require working with museum management to obtain permission. The permission might limit who the video could be shown to, but in the case of non-profits like schools, permission should not be a big problem. There may be some limitations on shooting, so that the production itself does not interfere with other visitors' enjoyment of the museum. I simply raise this as a caution, so you're not caught unaware, perhaps by having a security guard interrupt your shoot in the museum.

The same kind of virtual tour might make sense any time we are preparing students for a field visit, whether to a museum, plant, lab, forest, or concert.

WHY VIDEO?

Video production has become inexpensive and within the reach of individuals, schools, or training departments. There are really two aspects to this cost reduction that we should pay attention to. First is the reduced cost for equipment and software, along with the ease of use of these products.

Low Cost of Equipment and Software

Good consumer-grade digital camcorders can be purchased for several hundred dollars. We'll later discuss what you need in a camcorder; the very cheapest will not do. They impose some serious limitations and are not even really suitable for shooting graduations, weddings, birthday parties, and other personal or family uses for which they are intended. We'll need to spend a little more, but far short of the multiple thousands we used to have to spend to get a camcorder worth using.

While we'll need some other equipment, the other major expenditure used to be for video editing software. Basic non-linear editing software is now free or, for significantly better software, inexpensive.

NOTE

Non-linear editing is the process used now to edit video. It's non-linear because the pieces of video can be accessed and assembled in any order. We do not need to fast-forward through the tape to find the scene or shot we want.

You will also need to spend some money for a tripod, microphones, and, possibly, lights. While all camcorders have built-in mics, those will not work as well as external mics that you can place nearer the sound source.

There are two foolproof indicators whether a videographer is a pro or an amateur. The use of external mics is one. The other is the use of a tripod. Pros use tripods whenever they can.

You've seen amateurs shooting video of graduations or weddings. They're holding the camcorder in one hand and watching the video on the flip-out LCD panel. If they ever show the video to anyone, the audience will be in danger of motion sickness because of the camera movement. It's essentially impossible to hold a camcorder still when using one hand. The tripod holds the camcorder steady, greatly improving the resulting video.

If you can't use a tripod for some reason, you can hold it steadier than the one-hander by using two hands—one on each side of the camcorder, braced against the body, with the camcorder held against your head. In that position, you'll use the eyepiece or viewfinder, rather than the flip-out screen. Later we'll demonstrate other ways of steadying the camera, but the one-hander isn't one of them.

Light is what we use to make video; we capture images formed by light. The light that's available in your location may not produce the best possible video, or it may be the wrong color or in the wrong place. We'll talk about lights in detail later, but at this point, you should know that you may need some lights to make good video.

My point in listing tripod, mics, and lights here is not that they cost a lot of money. They don't. We're probably talking something under $500 for them. Other costs have come down much faster than these costs, so now we find that these formerly relatively small costs loom larger in comparison to camcorders and non-linear editing software.

Reduced Expectations of Quality

People now like to watch videos on YouTube and other video-sharing sites. The video there is often of poor quality compared to what we expect on cable or broadcast TV or professionally produced video. It may be poorly exposed, out of focus, unedited, or snowy. Yet people are happy with it and pass the links around to friends. At the same time, broadcast and cable TV, commercials, and professionally produced training videos continue to strive for high production values.

What does this popularity tell us about expectations of video quality? At this point I think it says we still need to try to achieve high-quality productions, but there are circumstances in which you may be able to get by with poorer quality. You may be able to use cell-phone quality video to make a point or convey a sense of immediacy. But in general, your audience will expect higher production values than cell phone clips for most purposes and may, in fact, discount the credibility of video that looks like it was hastily and cheaply produced. If it wasn't worth your time to make it look and sound good, is it worth their time to watch it?

TRAPS FOR THE UNWARY

After reading this far, you may be sold on the idea that you can produce video and that you should do so. Some of us have called this stage, "uninformed optimism." It's the first stage of a project, followed by "informed pessimism." As you learn more about video, or perhaps try a project, you begin to realize that producing good video is hard work. That realization may hit you on the third day of editing a five-minute video. Some parts of this are time-consuming; others are hard work.

The third part of the cycle is "informed optimism," as you and your team see what you have to do to finish and gain confidence that you can do it.

That's the first trap: not recognizing the time and effort that will go into a well-produced video. The second is related, but different. It's taking on a project that really is beyond your capabilities.

Some video should be left to professionals. A video of a concert, for example, is very demanding work. You can't start and stop your camcorder and expect to put compelling video together in edit. If you leave your camcorder running, you can't get the different shots you'll want to pick out the soloists or show cut-aways of the audience.

You will need multiple cameras and professional tools that maintain synchronization between video and sound at all times. To record a concert, you would need dual system recording, that is, one dedicated system for sound and cameras for the video. But note that, in a concert, the sound and video must be played in sync or things don't look right. The guitarist isn't strumming in rhythm, or the pianist is playing the wrong keys. Even if you're not a musician, you'll know that things don't look right. That's not something you can fix in edit.

If all you're trying to record is your child's solo, you can do that with your camcorder. But you won't get adequate video of a whole concert.

In this chapter, we have reviewed some of the reasons to use video, including reduced costs of the equipment and software necessary to produce video and improved ease of use compared to past production tools. We have also looked at some typical uses of video for the teacher or trainer. And finally, we've noted some traps to watch out for.

In the next chapter, we walk through the overall video production process.

Note: The change cycle is shown at http://changingminds.org/disciplines/change_management/psychology_change/positive_change.htm

CHAPTER

2

ONE TIME THROUGH THE PROCESS—A 30,000-FOOT VIEW

Before we start with video, let's take a step back and look at a design and development process for multimedia generally. If you understand the process described here, you'll see how the production of video fits into a larger process. When we're producing digital video for learning, it is rarely the case that we're producing fifteen- or thirty-minute videos, used like movies in the old days of instructional film. Most often now, we're using shorter video clips within a larger production, typically a website. We do that because using several media gives us flexibility in budget and time to use each medium for what it does best. Static images do some things really well, and they cost significantly less than thirty seconds of video showing the same image, which is the way we would have shown it in the old days of being limited to film.

You may be familiar with the ADDIE model for instructional design and development. It's an acronym for Analysis, Design, Development, Implementation, and Evaluation. These are the classic five stages of an instructional project. They're often represented in a flow chart or box diagram of some sort, looking something like the one in Figure 2.1.

While the model suggests that the phases are independent and sequential, in practice they are not (Gustafson & Branch, 2007). While a project will generally move from an

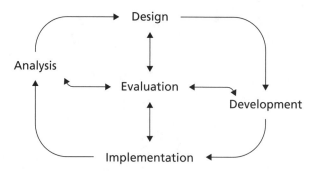

FIGURE 2.1. *The ADDIE Model.*

emphasis on Analysis activities, to more Design activities, to Development, and so on, at many points it is common to cycle back and re-visit decisions made earlier as we get further into the detail and reality of a project. For example, it may happen that, while in Development (actually creating the learning materials or media students or teachers will use), you learn more detail about the content that may challenge some aspect of Design decisions, or even Analysis. This moving back and forth among phases is to be expected, although it can be frustrating to project managers.

Since the Analysis phase is one in which decisions might be made about whether there is even a training or learning problem, the video production process usually doesn't have any impact there. We really start with Design, particularly in current uses of the models, which incorporate prototypes. Traditionally, the Design phase includes definitions of scope, content, and sequence. We will also make media decisions in Design, such as what media we will use. Note the plural. In multimedia development, we have a wide variety of media available to use: graphics, text, audio, and video are all possibilities. These media are useful in self-study web or e-learning courses and in instructor-led classroom and online learning. If video is selected as an appropriate medium, we follow a process something like that shown in Figure 2.2, which assumes video in the context of a website, a common and very flexible way to work.

I recommend developing prototypes during the Design phase, which would include producing some video. Prototypes are demonstrations of portions of the instructional product. Traditional Design phase deliverables include a design document, which is a description of what will be developed. Prototypes show what will be developed, rather than merely telling. As such they communicate intent much more clearly than a design document and allow the team to try out their processes for creating the media. In the training world, verifying the process helps create more reliable estimates of cost and time. In the academic world, verifying the process helps us make sure it is within our capabilities and budget.

In this way, note that Design and Development overlap, since we are developing media that students will use, but doing so during the Design phase.

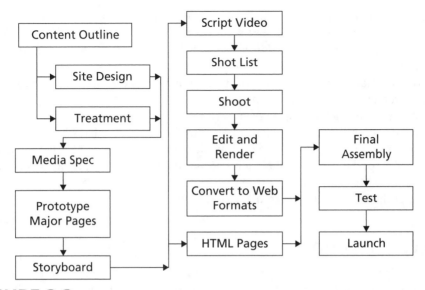

FIGURE 2.2. *Overall Process Flow.*

The chart in Figure 2.2 assumes some activities of Design are completed, specifically defining the content and objectives and specifying media, including the web and video.

The content outline lists, in a hierarchical fashion, the content to be included in the module. It should include subpoints for major topics, if not sub-subpoints. You will need that level of detail in later steps. The Site Design stage defines overall site layout and navigation, including whether the structure is tree, web, linear, or some combination.

TREATMENT

The Treatment stage includes any storyline, characters (such as avatars representing a teacher and students, or a learning coach), and how they will interact with the content.

> ## NOTE
>
> Mayer (2009) recommends personalizing multimedia. This principle includes writing in a less formal style and using the second person ("you") to refer to the learner. Such a style implicitly places the module in the role of a teacher, facilitator, or coach. Mayer further recommends use of an on-screen coach or visible author, making explicit who is behind the instruction (Clark & Mayer, 2008).

A storyline is a narrative that integrates the content to be presented. People learn from stories. The narrative might be as simple as setting a chemistry lesson as an experiment to answer a question. Jonassen (20014) and Merrill (2002) both advocate setting a problem to be solved as the context for learning. The treatment can include the setup of a problem and putting the instruction in the context of resources needed to solve that problem or class of problems.

Characters may include the person performing the experiment or an on-screen coach. In creating our video, we can script an introduction and conclusion in which we see the on-screen coach speaking, and use voice-over narration (we hear the voice but do not see the speaker) through the main body of the video. This technique simplifies editing, because we don't need to worry about maintaining synchronization between the visual of the speaker and his or her voice.

MEDIA SPECIFICATION

The Media Spec takes the teaching points listed in the content outline and defines the media to be used for each one. Recall that in these multimedia modules we have a variety of media available to us. Consider the nature of the content and decide the best way to depict it. Does it require graphics, as would be the case for geography? Is text appropriate, as in a discussion of a theory? Or do we need motion to describe a physics demonstration? We have the option to use more than one medium and the research to indicate the multiple presentations can reinforce each other. See the chart below.

Silk screening demonstration	On screen	Voice-over notes for script	Graphic	Video	Animation
Show the process of creating the screen	Title: Prepare the screen				
	Dissolve to show animation				35-second animation of process with voice-over

Silk screening demonstration	On screen	Voice-over notes for script	Graphic	Video	Animation
1. Draw image on tracing paper	Title: The image can be drawn, photocopied, or printed	Draw image on tracing paper or clear acetate. The area to be inked must be opaque.	Photo		
2. Attach tracing paper to emulsion	Title: Use darkroom	Attach the image to screen on emulsion side		15-second video, darkened to look like darkroom	
3. Expose emulsion to UV light	Title: Use darkroom	Expose the emulsion to UV light to prepare screen	Photo		
4. Rinse emulsion		Rinse the emulsion. The areas not exposed to light will wash away to show the image.		10-sec video	
Review	(List steps)	Review steps	Use still from animation		

In the example, the designer has chosen to use several media to demonstrate how to make a screen for silk screen printing. The left column lists the teaching points from the outline. The other columns list the media available. For the overview, the title of the segment will display, followed by an animation of the whole process. Then we go step-by step, using a still image to show someone drawing the image, with text to indicate alternative ways to prepare the image. We use a still image here rather than more expensive video because the drawing of the image is not a major learning outcome. We need an image; drawing it is one way to create it, but others will work. The learning outcomes are related to the silk screen process.

For the points in which motion is important, we show video clips to demonstrate attaching the image to the screen and the thorough rinse needed to wash away the unexposed emulsion.

It may be worth noting why the designer chose to use an animation where she did, for the overall process. Some parts of the process are really hard to photograph or video because they occur at a very small scale or in the dark. Drawings would work to show the sequence of exposing the screen, then washing away the emulsion, but an animation can emphasize certain aspects that students sometimes get confused, such as which part of the emulsion washes away—the exposed or unexposed.

NOTE

Teachers or trainers familiar with other media may be surprised at the level of detail required here. Because we are dealing with video and other media, and sometimes teams of people, we have more choices. It is really important to document decisions so that when you come back to put this segment together, you have all the assets (images, animation, video, photos) you need to make the module work as intended. Yes, it's more detail. And yes, it pays off to plan at this level of detail.

PROTOTYPES

I mentioned earlier that I find prototypes to be more useful than design documents in communicating intent or design decisions. Here's where we put this idea to work. Using pencil and paper, a draw program, or even PowerPoint, create the look and feel of certain key pages in the module. Consider the appearance of title pages, menus, pages that present information as video, text, and graphics, and those that provide for student practice, including questions or practice exercises. Initially, we're concerned with appearance: colors, page layout, placement of menus or other navigation features, and type size and font.

The first drafts of prototypes may be predictable, even trite in their appearance. Get beyond those; expand your thinking, try some new looks. By the third or fourth draft prototype, you may be onto something really interesting.

Once you have settled on look and feel, perhaps by combining elements from two or three designs, you're ready to try to make these prototypes work. You move from appearance prototypes to functional or technical prototypes. Now you're trying to demonstrate that you know how to use the authoring tools to create all the interactions and displays on your pages.

You may ask, Why are we doing all this development now? This is the Design phase. Yes, it is. But we need to make sure we know how to make it all work before we commit to specific features. We also need to know how long it takes to make it work, to see whether our time and budget allow.

When we are creating the prototypes, we don't have actual video or graphics assets, or even text. Use placeholders for these. You can use video and graphics from previous work or samples from the web (be careful about copyrights). For text, use so-called Greek text, which is meaningless, Latin-looking text commonly beginning "Lorem ipsum dolor sit amet, consectetur adipisicing elit, . . ." These placeholders occupy the space used for your content without requiring actual content. Besides saving time, the use of these placeholders lets reviewers concentrate on screen appearance and function, rather than content or meaning.

Since one use of prototypes is to have something to try out with our learners, these prototypes allow us to prove out the product (with our learners) and the process (with our developers). Once we have tested the appearance and the process, we can commit to developing the whole module with some degree of confidence.

SCRIPT SITE

Create a script covering the whole website. This single document includes all verbal and visual content, although normally the visual content is described in words rather than shown as visuals.

The two-column script is the format used in multimedia production. This format places all visual information in the left column and audio in the right. So titles, scene appearance, and action, all visual elements, are on the left side and dialog is on the right, as seen in Figure 2.3.

A convention carried over from television is to use all caps for the dialog. I do not recommend all caps because it is known to be harder to read. Normal sentence case works well.

Also note that, when typing a script using your word processor, do not use the column format. You need to keep the adjacent left and right column information together. Use a table, but omit most horizontal lines. Use the horizontal lines (rules) between scenes and shots, but not within them. Or you can use script software, such as Celtx, to generate a two-column script. Celtx is specifically designed for video scripts, so adapting it for multimedia websites may be a challenge. That's what I used to prepare this sample script.

VIDEO	AUDIO
MEDIUM: Exterior. cook removes cooked flatbread from grill, using tongs, place on plate. Flatbread has distinct grill marks	COOK: Today we're going to grill flatbread, one of humankind's oldest styles of bread, and one of the easiest to make.
MASTER: cook in kitchen, behind table,	COOK: The dough is a simple yeast bread dough. You can make it easily
CLOSE UP: pizza dough in bag	or buy pizza crust dough from the grocery store
MEDIUM: cook behind table	COOK: Because this is a simple dough, I'll show you how to make it from scratch.
CLOSE UP: cook	COOK: Some people get nervous about yeast doughs, but they are really very forgiving and are mostly about waiting while the yeast does its work.
MEDIUM: cook behind table	COOK: We'll just make a small batch, enough for four flatbreads.
CLOSE UP: table top–follow action	COOK (VO) You'll need flour, yeast, water, and a little olive oil. You may add some herbs to the dough, such as herbs de Provence.

FIGURE 2.3. *Two-Column Script.*

You will want to add shot numbers to the script. These will be useful in tracking video while you are shooting and later in editing.

CONCURRENT WORK

The flowchart splits here. Some of the team does the detail work on the video, while others work on the other assets for the website or other container for the module. If you are working by yourself, then you'll sequence the work any way that you find productive, although when you're shooting video you will need more people.

Shot List

The shot list is derived from the script. It is one of several script breakdowns. You can think of it as reordering the script to reflect the order in which you want to shoot the video. You do not shoot the video in the order in which it is to be viewed. There are several reasons for this, starting from the logistics of shooting.

When you are demonstrating a process, shooting an interview, or creating the kickoff episode for a case study, your script should list a variety of shots, some close-ups, some medium shots, or, in the case of dialog, some shots of each participant.

Each of these kinds of shots requires a different setup, whether in the studio or on location. Lights will need to be set differently, for example, for your close-ups than for the medium or cover shots. In the dialog set, the lights will be set up differently for each party in the dialog. You do not want to change the lights any more than you need to, or cause unnecessary delays in the shoot. So you'll set up for the medium or cover shot of the demonstration, or for the interviewees, whose times may be more constrained than that of the interviewer. Shoot all of the video you need for each setup, then stop, send the talent on break, and set up the lights and camcorder for the close-ups of the interviewer. Then shoot again. That's right. You're often shooting the same scene twice or more.

Consider the interview or dialog setup, shown in Figure 2.4. Maybe you're interviewing a noted expert, your dean, or someone playing a role in a management case study. The dean and the expert may have very tight schedules, allowing limited shooting time. Shoot the whole interview or dialog with the camera on that key person. Then, after setting up for the reverse shot, shoot the scene with the camera on the interviewer, who is now just asking the questions. You'll also shoot some reaction shots, which I describe below.

The Shoot

Shot list and script in hand, you head to your location with your team and equipment. You've visited the location already to make sure you know where the power outlets are and you've gotten permission from the person in charge. You've figured out lighting. It's all planned.

Then, after your first shoot, you've captured the person's comments with a face shot that you can use as your most common shot in the final video. Now move the camera around to get a face shot of the interviewer or the other person in the dialog. Adjust the lights for that person, and record the questions, comments, and even shots of the person just listening, paying rapt attention, or looking confused, quizzical, or even angry, if that's appropriate for the story. Later, in edit, you can use those shots of the interviewer or other person in the dialog to break up the overall video and cut out

FIGURE 2.4.   *Over the Shoulder (OTS) Dialog Setup.*

sections of the interviewee's speech that don't contribute so much to the final video. We'll talk more about editing later; suffice it to say now that when you cut out speech, you'll need other video to cover the edit visually.

The extra video you shoot that is not of the main subject is called B-roll. Naturally, the video of the subject is called A-roll. Use the B-roll video to cover edits. Say you got forty-five seconds of your person speaking on A-roll, and it's all very coherent and clear. Yet in the middle, the person is briefly distracted and needs to pause and start over. If you just edit out the bad few seconds, you will likely have a jump cut, a visual mismatch between two very similar frames, which gives the appearance of a jump. In edit, you will edit the video and audio to clean up the narrative, then lock the audio track and replace a little of the video before the jump cut with B-roll of the other person listening. Voila! No jump cut.

EDIT

Once you and your talent shoot the video, you need to edit it. Editing can be very time-consuming. You edit to put the video in the right sequence, remove errors, select the best video of that you shot to tell your story, improve the pace, and add sound effects, music, or visual effects, such as transitions.

To make edit go as smoothly as possible, you first want to review all your video and sound assets. Write down which ones you want to use. Professional videographers slate each shot, that is, record a few seconds of a small whiteboard, on which is written scene and take number, as well as time codes if your equipment provides reliable ones. Use these slates to list shots in your edit decision list. This list will grow to include how you want to trim shots, sequence them, and add cut-ins and cut-aways.

NOTE

Defining Cut-In and Cut-Away

A cut-in is a close-up shot showing a detail of the main subject. A cut-away is a shot of something other than the main subject, used to show a reaction, the setting, context, or perhaps something the dialog refers to.

Once you have made the editing decisions, recorded on the edit decision list, you can begin the actual edit. Our non-linear editors are very forgiving. If you make a bad edit, you can simply undo it and try again. Follow the edit decision list to assemble the shots you want; trim them to improve pace and the story. Insert cut-ins and cut-aways. And add sounds and special effects. It's easy to describe, but time-consuming to actually do.

SITE CONSTRUCTION—HTML PAGES

At the same time, as video production moves along, development of the website can continue. The website will contain all of the content and student activities, including the video. Since video is the most time-consuming part of the development process, part of the team may work on that while others work on the site itself, if you are doing this as a team. If you're working by yourself, you've got some challenges ahead, but it can be done.

In this book, which is primarily about digital video, I won't go into much detail about constructing the site. I can say that you don't need to wait for video to develop the site. You should develop using templates or CSS style sheets that control the appearance of pages, so pages with similar functions look the same. That is, all pages that display video should have the same look and function. Pages that ask questions or set up problems should look and act similar to each other, and to the pages for video.

In addition to video, you will have text and graphics, and maybe some animations. You can also be developing these while video production is going on.

Construct pages with placeholders for as-yet-unfinished art or video, then simply replace the placeholders with the actual assets as they become available. If you are building learning interactions and you're not sure exactly how to make them work, you can be trying and testing so they're ready by the time the other work is done.

FINAL ASSEMBLY AND TEST

What's left to do is put it all together. As video, audio, and web assets are completed, assemble the finished multimedia website. Bring in finished video, load it to the development server, change html pages and components to point to the real video instead of the placeholders, and make sure it all works.

NOTE

It's good practice to have two nearly identical web servers. They should run the same operating system and server software. One is the development server. This server may not have the same hardware and level of reliability as the production server. The development server is where work in progress goes first, to be tested. It may not even be available to the World Wide Web, but only inside the development group.

The other is the production server. Finished, tested, reliable work goes here. This is the server available to the World Wide Web. This server probably has regular backups, first-rate hardware, and an uninterruptible power supply.

Testing consists of fully exercising everything on the website as it is supposed to work, and making sure it doesn't misbehave if users do something unpredictable. What happens if learners enter unexpected responses? Does the feedback and scoring still work as intended? What happens if they click where we didn't intend them to click?

We'll go through stages of testing before releasing the site to our intended audience. We want to make sure it works technically and instructionally. These really require separate testing regimens, one technical and one for learning.

LAUNCH AND DISTRIBUTION

Our final step is distribution, making the content available to our audience. Most often this will be via a website. "If you build it they will come" is a fine strategy for a baseball movie, but not for an instructional website. You will need a communications or marketing effort, and in some cases a change management process.

We have walked through the whole process in this chapter, from planning to distribution. We've emphasized those steps that are really critical to making your production work, such as scripting, storyboarding, and editing.

Some sections will receive much more detailed treatment in subsequent chapters; others will not. The difference is really about the focus of this book. Our focus is on creating digital video for learning. Those aspects of the whole process that are better dealt with elsewhere, such as web development or change management, get only cursory treatment here. You may already know those things or we will refer you to other sources.

Next we get into the detail of video production. We'll start with planning. As a former client reminded me, the basic process is "plan before do." This is nowhere more important than in video production because of all the different pieces you need to keep track of and sequence to make the best use of your limited time and resources.

CHAPTER

3

PLANNING

"Plan before do."

—Senior project manager

One common mistake among beginning video producers is to shoot before planning exactly what they want to do. The result is, predictably, poor video, bordering on useless. More to the point, the planning needs to be concerned with what the viewer is intended to take away from the production. Beginning with the end in mind will vastly improve the production.

The planning stage also is an opportunity to bring the team together to create a shared understanding of what the video is to accomplish and how it will achieve it. Creating good video is not a solo effort. The team will achieve much more than any one of us can alone.

GOALS AND OBJECTIVES

While I am an instructional designer by profession, I don't write standard Mager-style objectives ("Given a chemistry lab setup and a sample of unknown concentration, the student will be able to perform a titration within 10 percent of nominal values"). Those objectives are so structured and jargony that students don't understand them. Designers understand them; students and subject-matter experts don't need them. We do need to have a clear, shared understanding of the knowledge or skill that should result from the instructional experience we are creating.

To a large extent, that means understanding how this learning fits into a curriculum or job expectations. There are some important general ideas that help this understanding. Most often, we don't expect our learners to learn *about* something. We want them to be able to *do* something. As David Jonassen (2004) has been known to say, No one gets paid to know about something. They get paid to do something, and that something is usually solving some kind of problem. We'll come back to that important idea in the next section.

The importance of agreeing on the goal of the instruction is that the whole team needs to have the same goals in mind. You will probably have to discuss the content to make sure there is a shared vision. The team will include a subject-matter expert (SME) who might be a teacher, skilled practitioner, or, in some cases, an analyst or developer responsible for a new system or business process. The SME is a prime source of knowledge for the training, but others on the team will have input to the understanding.

NOTE

Note that training is not always on a topic, process, or system that exists already. In corporate training, you will often be required to create training for something that doesn't yet exist, but is coming and under development. The training has to be ready before the new process or system is ready so people can perform on the first day.

It is important for all to understand that such training is necessarily a best guess as to what will be the best way to work. As any new process or system comes into use, it will change and people will find better ways to use it than were originally planned. The training should remain current, meaning that new systems often require significant revisions to training after a year or so of use.

The shared understanding of the goal makes the process run more smoothly and effectively. The script writer, camera operator/director of photography, web developer, video editor, and designer all come to the project with the same understanding of the learning goal, so their decisions all move the project in the same direction.

ID CONSIDERATIONS—FIRST PRINCIPLES, SOLVING PROBLEMS

David Merrill's First Principles (2002) and David Jonassen's *Learning to Solve Problems* (2004) approach instructional design very differently, but share an important concept: Instruction should be problem-centered. That is, what we most often are teaching people to do is to solve problems. In the corporate world, the problems might be related to how a customer service representative handles calls from customers. A physics teacher wants students to be able to calculate the force needed to accelerate a baseball by some amount. A health educator wants diabetes patients to be able to plan menus to maintain blood sugar levels. These are all real-world problems.

The importance of these problems as the goal of instruction is that they provide a context for the content. Without the problem, the knowledge a learner gains may be inert, that is, not retrievable when needed.

Let's say John "learns" the hundreds of policies governing refunds at the online store he works at as a customer service representative (CSR). He can answer questions about the policies. Policies are always phrased as general rules, so they apply broadly. Yes, there are exceptions, but even here, they apply to many situations.

Then John starts answering phones and makes many errors, along with upsetting some customers. Real customers don't call about general policies. They call about a $3.25 overcharge, or a medium size shipped when she needed a small. The policies were taught in isolation, not in the context of real problems presented by customers, so he wasn't able to accurately and quickly apply what he had learned in the real situation.

How should the training have been organized to improve John's performance on the job? I'll describe a somewhat simplified approach, concentrating on the core of the instructional design. Let's assume that Susan already knows how to look up an order on the computer.

We'll start with the problem, and then continue with other aspects of Merrill's First Principles (Figure 3.1).

Begin by showing a customer service representative, Susan, in a cubicle, answering a call. The audio includes both sides of the conversation. We hear Susan answer the call, and a customer says she doesn't understand the charge for shipping on her last purchase. She thought it was supposed to be free shipping.

The phone call sets up the problem. Another part of First Principles calls for activation of prior learning. Our learner has previously learned to look up orders. We remind her that she needs to identify the customer and look up the order.

The dialog continues with Susan asking some questions to identify the customer and order so she can look it up. She finds the order. Then we demonstrate the new skill or performance.

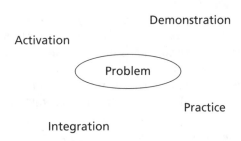

FIGURE 3.1. *First Principles.*

Now we show the order history screen, so the learner can see what Susan is paying attention to. Direct the learner's attention to the key information on the screen, which in this case is the shipping charge and the order total, since whether shipping is free depends on the total order amount.

Only now do we go to the policy, since the learner has a problem to solve: What should the shipping charge be? Explaining the relevant policy in the context of the phone call will make it easier for the learner to recall and apply the policies correctly on the job.

The next step is to have the learner practice what we have just demonstrated. So we start a new problem, on the same policy, but this time ask the learner has to choose the appropriate response. The new problem should be similar, but not identical.

Of course, we have much more to know than just the policy on shipping charges. Some policies are more complex than others, and in some cases more than one policy may apply to a specific circumstance.

We started the program with a fairly simple call, easily resolved with use of one policy. Subsequent calls will become more difficult, requiring interpretation. Some may require the CSR to use some discretion, as he is allowed to waive some charges for goodwill or to retain a customer.

As the calls grow more difficult, we will also intersperse calls requiring application of policies from earlier in the course. The learner also needs to figure out which policy to apply, so we won't make all the calls in one module apply to the same policy or group of policies.

This moving from one policy to additional policies, following the same instructional pattern, integrates the new knowledge and skill into real-world activities, the last step in First Principles.

Assessment of learning will come in the form of a quiz. The quiz will follow the same format as the instruction, with each episode beginning with a phone call. The learner chooses which policy applies and selects a response to the customer. Part of the quiz is asking the learner why he or she chose that response, to help reinforce the use of the policies in meeting customer needs.

Admittedly, this approach is quite different from traditional training. We set the knowledge of the policies in the context of answering calls, so that the knowledge is readily retrievable in the job context.

We should also note here that there are times you won't use this design exactly. Sometimes you're helping people learn a procedure, such as performing a lab experiment in chemistry, baking bread, or replacing parts in a computer. These procedural modules may be used as just-in-time training, so the learner or user supplies the problem and context. They go to the training when they need it. The rest of the strategy, activation of prior learning, demonstration, application, and integration, will be appropriate and useful.

This design might be inappropriate in a performance support system. In that case, the user supplies the context. One support system you may be familiar with is the software used to prepare income tax returns. Most often the user is not trying to learn how to prepare a return, just to complete it accurately. The videos in that software are there to demonstrate what to do or which forms to complete. The problem is in the context itself: to complete the income tax return. It doesn't need to be stated in each part of the software.

The team needs to have a common understanding of the intended design, as well as the goal of the instruction. Most often the design is centered around a problem. This focus on solving problems drives every aspect of the production, from scripting through editing and distribution.

INTEGRATING VIDEO WITH OTHER MEDIA

The design we've been talking about in this chapter need not be implemented entirely in video. We have inexpensive technologies to use along with video. I love video, of course. That's why I wrote this book. But it's not for everything. Most often now, we're writing instruction for the web or at least for use within a PowerPoint presentation. (Section V of this book, beginning with Chapter 21, goes into detail on how to integrate different media.)

Start with the understanding that, even though video is well within your reach, it is usually more time-consuming to create video than other, static media. Let's further assume, for the sake of the example, that we're targeting web delivery. We could, for instance, create the whole thing as video, including static pages. But that's really extra effort for no benefit. It's usually easier to create a text page as a web page rather than as a video frame. You also have the benefit that it's easy for the learner to control the pace with a web page. That is, the page does not advance until the learner chooses to go to the next page. Easy on the web, not so much on video. Learner control of pace is known to be of benefit to the learner (Clark & Mayer, 2008).

On the web, we're basically constructing a website with some pages that include video. The video may account for a large part of the student time in the site, but playing a video of any length requires only a single web page.

You can think of the web page as a container for whatever content we want to put on it, whether text, graphics, video, sound, or anything else.

Let's walk back through the design for the customer service training to see how we use video and where we use other media. The module should open with a title page and an introduction. These can be text and graphics on a web page. The introduction describes the setting and connects this module to previous ones in which the learners have already learned to retrieve orders. In the problem setup, in which our character, Susan, answers the phone call, we can use video. We hear both sides of the conversation. A convention that works well is to use an audio filter on the customer's over-the-phone voice so it sounds like a phone call, while we hear Susan's voice unfiltered. You'll modify the sound in the edit phase. Record the audio in full fidelity and then change it later. (See the instructional sequence in Figure 3.2, described below.)

Susan answers the call, acknowledges the customer's concern.

- IDENTIFY ORDER
- RETRIEVE ORDER ON COMPUTER

Susan recalls the procedure to access the customer's order.

ORDER NUMBER: 6BY70421
DATE: 08/11/11
CUSTOMER: PAULSON, W. G.

ITEMS:

SHIPPING: $7.00
TOTAL: $38.14

The computer screen showing the customer's order, including the shipping charges.

FREE SHIPPING ON USA
ORDERS $50.00 OR OVER

Susan recalls the policy on shipping charges and tells the customer why there was a charge on her order.

FIGURE 3.2. *Storyboard: Instructional Sequence.*

When Susan goes to the system to look up the order, we can use a screen recorder like Camtasia or Captivate, rather than pointing the camera at the screen. The results will be much clearer images of the screen.

When we want to bring in the appropriate policy, we'll go back to text on a web page. It's easy to do and, more important, easy to modify later should some detail of the policy change. A voice-over narration can explain why that policy applies and how it applies in the specific case. Then we can go back to video to see Susan explaining the policy to the customer. If Susan needs to make an adjustment, a screen recorder will show the system screens, while we hear the dialog.

That description carries us through the problem, activation of prior learning, and the demonstration. Now we want the student to practice, so things will be a little different.

Again, we can use a video to set up the problem. We can use a screen simulation to have the learner find the account, because he or she has learned to do that already. That simulation can be done in HTML or using a program like Adobe Captivate. Once the learner displays the correct order screen, the learner can choose a response to the customer or review the policy first and then respond. The response will be a multiple-choice question, to keep things simple. When the learner chooses a response, we can go to video to see Susan say that response and hear the customer's reply.

Integration of the new knowledge, by means of successive problems and policies, follows the same media pattern. We use video where we want to show motion and sound, static text and graphics where we don't need motion, voice-over narration when we have visual and verbal information, and questions set up on web pages, sometimes with video or audio feedback.

Sometimes the video may provide only the demonstration part of the First Principles model. Consider a common problem in chemistry classes: Students go into a lab without really understanding what it is they are supposed to do, since they've never done it before. The instructor sets up the problem the students are to solve prior to the lab and links the lab problem to prior knowledge. Then we use a video to demonstrate the lab procedure. The video might be available on the web so students can study it prior to coming to the lab. Once in the lab, students go through the procedure (practice) and then meet again with the instructor to integrate the new learning into their knowledge of chemistry.

STORY AND CHARACTER

In the instructional design section we just finished, I gave the characters names, John and Susan. Partly that was to ease the writing of the section, since I didn't then have to repeat titles (customer service representative, for example) or descriptions. The names should also help you, the reader, keep track of who I'm talking about at any point. These are the basics of a simple story. John needs to learn something and has had some preventable difficulty. Susan is a CSR in our training scenarios demonstrating a skill.

Mayer's Personalization Principle (Clark & Mayer, 2012) addresses this topic well. His research tells us that people learn better when the writing is in a conversational rather than formal style and when we use a learning agent in the multimedia. We'll talk about writing style in the next chapter. Here we'll talk about the use of a learning agent or coach.

A lot, probably most, web-based instruction that currently exists doesn't seem to be associated with a person. Text or disembodied voices convey content, but the learner has no idea who this knowledge or content is coming from. Mayer's studies direct us to include a character in the instruction that can be understood to be the one telling or talking to the learner. It does not have to be a real person. It doesn't even have to be a person. One student project created a graphic of a microphone with a face and arms, named Mike R. Phone (Figure 3.3). Mike included a button that played or stopped the voice-over narration on the subject of writing and recording announcements for a school. There is a link to that production on the book's website.

If budget and time allow, it can be a real person. The person does not have to be visible on screen at all times. It can work well to begin with a video segment that includes the learning agent, then proceed with voice-over, in which the learning agent is not visible. Then conclude with the agent on-screen again. A higher budget production,

FIGURE 3.3. *Mike R. Phone.*

By Patty Howard, used by permission.

using more video, can have the agent on-screen through most of the module, perhaps shot using green-screen (see Chapter 13) so the agent can be placed in any setting or even in an existing graphic or image.

You will learn that voice-over is considerably easier to edit than talent-on-camera (TOC) video (in which the person speaking is shown on the screen), so keep that in mind in planning.

Mayer's Personalization Principle leads us to use a learning agent in our productions. What's the importance of a story?

People learn from and remember stories better than isolated facts and concepts. Particularly if you're dealing with content that can be personal, such as diversity training or even how to do a performance review, creating a story to involve the learner will enhance learning.

The Abilene Paradox is a commercial video (see the link on the book's website) that uses a story to help people understand how to deal with agreement, not disagreement. There are many examples of such use of stories to help people learn and remember important skills. Another is *Michael and Lisa* (link on the website) used in a diversity course, also professionally produced.

Writing stories to engage the learner is more difficult than simply telling, but may be worth doing. The story works because emotions are involved, the learner cares about the characters, and the dramatic arc keeps the learner engaged. The dramatic arc or structure, as you may recall, sets up a situation, raises tension by introducing complications or conflict, reaches a climax, then falling action, in which the main conflict is resolved, then finally the resolution or denouement.

Writing a good story may be more challenging than writing expository training, but there are writers who can do it well—and it is worth the extra time. The video production is more challenging, but would be a good project to take on when you have some experience with more didactic approaches.

■ ■ ■

Once we have planned our video and accompanying content and made sure we have agreement on goals, design, character, and story, it's time to write. The next chapter works through that crucial activity.

CHAPTER

4

WRITING THE SCRIPT

The planning in the previous chapter leads to an actual script. What had been outlines and descriptions starts to take on details and images as the writer develops the actual words students will read and hear. A well-written script brings the content alive so that it can be recorded and created in tangible form as spoken language and visuals. It's the script that guides the rest of content development.

I recommend scripting the whole project including, obviously, the video, but also any accompanying web pages, animation, or other content. For the content reviewers, seeing it all in one document helps them understand the flow and logic and make sure nothing is missing or unnecessarily duplicated or explained in a sequence that is confusing to the learner. For the video producers, web developers, graphic artists, and other developers, seeing their parts in the context of the whole project helps clarify what their part contributes and how it fits into the whole.

In this chapter we will go through the process of writing a script, including organization, treatment, and writing style, the use of a style guide, and, finally, breaking down the script in ways that make it useful for those with particular needs later in the production process.

ORGANIZATION

The script, in effect, sets out the instructional strategy and sequence of the project. The sequence content as presented must make sense to the learner and must lead to learning. Some common organizational themes are listed here:

■ *Chronological*—Useful in conveying content that has time as an organizer, such as historical events, biological evolution, and geology, among others. A timeline is a useful organizing metaphor.

■ *Sequential*—Closely related to chronological, but on shorter time scales or when the sequence is part of a procedure the learner needs to master. In this case the learner has to perform a series of tasks in sequence, rather than observing a chronology of events outside of his or her control. A list of steps or a flowchart may help the learner visualize the sequence.

■ *Simple to complex*—When teaching a new concept, begin with the simplest, most obvious example. If we're teaching about birds, begin with a robin or sparrow rather than a penguin or ostrich. Elaborate on the concept, moving to the more complex, less obvious examples.

■ *Whole-part-whole*—When dealing with complicated ideas or procedures, start with a simplified definition, summary, or example of the whole idea. Then decompose it and go through the parts of the idea. Finally, bring all the parts back together to look at the whole, in a more sophisticated, complex view. This book basically follows this organizing principle, with the whole presented in Chapter 2, and then going through the details. We'll bring it all back together in Chapter 23.

■ *Known to unknown*—Start with what the learners already know about the subject. Perhaps it is useful to remind them what they learned in a previous module or course. Then build on that knowledge by introducing new content that is related to what they already know.

Note that these organizational themes are not mutually exclusive. The whole course might use a whole-part-whole organization, while modules within the course use sequential, simple to complex, or known to unknown organization.

TREATMENT

We begin writing with the treatment. This step is borrowed from the film business, in which the treatment, usually about one-third to one-half the length of the final script, tells the whole story in a narrative style. Screenwriters and aspiring film makers use the treatment as part of the proposal for funding. We won't use it that way, but it's still a useful step in developing the script. The treatment, in a narrative or outline form, describes the entire production from the point of view of the learner. See the sample below.

Sample Treatment

The opening screen includes the title and a stylized drawing of a wrench, with a face. The wrench begins to speak, introducing himself as Tommy, who will be the guide through this module on basic hand tools. Tommy explains that the learner may click the sound on or off or choose to view the written narrative rather than listen.

After Tommy begins to speak, the Next button appears in the lower right.

On the next screen a menu appears, as a series of pictures and name of tools. Tommy says that the learner may click on any tool to see how it is used. Clicking on any tool image or name takes the learner to a screen. . . .

This brief sample of a treatment illustrates several important points about a treatment. It is written in present tense. It describes what the learner sees and hears, as well as what options are available on the screen. It does not include word-for-word narration, but only the summary content of the narration. The actual script will be more verbose.

Different members of the team will use the treatment in different ways. The graphic artist will start noting the required graphics, including the animated hammer. The audio person will note the need to record voice-over narration. The web developer will see various links and buttons to create, as well as the need to incorporate the animation and sound.

All of them will review the treatment and offer suggestions. The graphic artist might suggest that it would be easier to use a pair of pliers instead of the hammer, because it could be animated with legs to move around the screen. The web developer might be concerned about the number of tools compared to the screen real estate, or whether the menu structure as described limits later development, if the team later wants to add more tools.

In these ways the treatment offers a platform for collaboration and discussion as the team improves on the vision the writer sets out.

FORMAT

Most often we will use a two-column script, as shown in Exhibit 4.1.

EXHIBIT 4.1

Sample Two-Column Script: Baking Yeast Bread

1. Family at dinner table—follow bread as it is passed	VO: It's wonderful to have homemade bread with a family dinner. It's not hard to make. Follow along with us as we make bread.
2. WS—Collette, Assemble ingredients and equipment	VO: Collette is going to help us bake our bread today.
3. MS—Assemble ingredients and recipe	We'll start by making sure we have everything we need, including the recipe.
4. ECU—recipe (We don't need to be able to read it)	The recipe has the amounts of each ingredient.
5. CU of each ingredient AP or bread flour Title: 3 cups	VO: All purpose or bread flour—either will work well in this recipe.
6. Whole wheat flour Title: 3 cups	VO: Traditional whole wheat flour
7. Sugar Title: 1 Tablespoon	VO: Sugar
8. Salt Title: ½ tsp	VO: A little salt
9. Instant or active dry yeast Title: 1 packet or 2 ¼ tsp.	VO: A packet of yeast
10. Measuring cup of water	VO: About 1 cup of warm water
11. CU—Talent checks dates on yeast (do not show actual date)	VO: Make sure the yeast is fresh. Check the expiration dates. Old ingredients will result in heavy bread.
12. CU—Sprinkle yeast on water	VO: Put the water in a large bowl and add the yeast to it.
13. Mix dry ingredients in mixing bowl	VO: Mix the dry ingredients in a mixing bowl.
14. MS—Pour dry ingredients into large bowl	VO: Add the dry ingredients to the bowl with the water and yeast.

The two-column format shows all the visual information in the left column and audio in the right. For that reason it's sometimes called the audio-visual format. It is the most commonly used format for instructional videos and multimedia, as well as news, documentaries, and commercials. Each shot is numbered.

The video column describes the shots and the content, but not in so much detail that the director has no freedom to shoot the video as he or she wants. At this point, the script is the writer's vision of the finished video. Here are some standard abbreviations used in this sample script:

- WS—Wide shot. Shows the context the video is in, in this case a kitchen in a home

- MS—Medium shot. Shows the talent in a waist shot, plus the work table and ingredients

- CU—Close-up. To see the detail of what the talent is doing or looking at

- ECU—Extreme close-up. In this script, we'll show the recipe, close enough that the viewer can see what it is.

The audio includes the abbreviation VO, for voice-over. The audio comes from an unseen narrator rather than the talent on camera. If the talent did the speaking, demonstrating the process, we would use TOC, meaning Talent on Camera. The script writer chose to use voice-over to simplify both shooting and editing. With amateur talent, getting the actions and speaking both right can be pretty demanding. The shoot is easier because we don't have to worry about extraneous sounds, as any recorded sounds can be removed in edit. The director can speak to the talent while shooting to reduce retakes (and waste of materials). Later, in edit, the spoken directions can be taken out.

Editing is simplified because the editors won't have to worry about keeping voice and lip movements in synchronization, since the talent on camera has no speaking role.

If there are several characters in the scene, the TOC would be replaced with the names of the characters, in caps, THOMAS. The use of caps differentiates the character name from spoken dialog. Actors will usually highlight their lines in the script.

Another script format is the single-column format, most often used for dramatic productions rather than instructional videos. There is a sample one-column script on the CV4TT website and many samples can be found on the web. But because it is so rarely used in instructional video, we will not include a sample here.

WRITING

A video is a visual and dramatic production, placing demands on the writer to show rather than tell and to engage the learner in the events unfolding on the screen.

The writer of the Michael and Lisa video on the *Creating Video for Teachers and Trainers* website follows the dramatic arc, setting up a conflict, which is seemingly resolved when Michael apologizes. His explanation of why he was upset changes the audience's sympathies, so that at the end of the video, the audience identifies with Lisa more than with Michael as he reveals his prejudices.

A simple narrated video with some visuals could have made the same point, but the story makes the Michael and Lisa video far more compelling. The audience's involvement in the story brings the concepts of diversity and inclusion alive.

This sample script in Exhibit 4.1 begins with (and ends with) a family at dinner, passing the bread. This device is intended to motivate the viewer to bake bread, by identifying with the family serving homemade bread at the table. The video will show how to bake bread, perhaps helping the viewer see that it's really not that difficult. Its inclusion here illustrates that the writer wants to think in terms of stories and emotional engagement, as well as the instruction. By ending with a similar scene, the writer pairs the opening and closing in a dramatically satisfying way.

Showing rather than telling, and following a few principles of multimedia, we arrive at some guidelines for writing style.

Write in Active Voice

Active voice is clearer about who is doing something, as well as being more explicit about what the learner is expected to do as a result of the instruction. Active voice usually requires fewer words to say the same thing. Here are examples of passive and active voice.

"Caution should be exercised when working around electricity." Compare that to "You should be careful when working with electricity" or even "Be careful when working with electricity."

Both sentences have the same meaning. But the second, in active voice, is much stronger and clearer. It is obvious that it is the learner who should be careful. In the first sentence, in passive voice, it's vague who should be cautious.

Writers sometimes use passive voice to avoid stating responsibility. The classic "Mistakes were made" kind of statement acknowledges errors without indicating who made the mistakes.

Writing in passive voice results in wooden prose that has no capacity to engage the learner.

Personalize the Writing

This recommendation echoes Mayer's Personalization Principle (Mayer, 2009), in which he says that a personal writing style enhances learning. Active voice is part of that style. But more than that, he recommends using a conversational style, not a formal academic style of writing, and addressing the learner as "you," rather than in the third person, "the learner" or "the viewer." It follows that the narrator or talent on camera would refer to him- or herself as "I" or "we." With these simple changes, what might have been a lecture becomes a conversation.

Using a conversational style allows the writer to let go of some formal writing while still being grammatically correct. This book is written in a conversational, informal style. While being accurate and crediting sources for my ideas, I have avoided a dry academic style that many of you would find less interesting or more difficult to understand.

Think Visually

Video is a visual medium. A script that calls for a lot of text on screen with a voice-over doesn't use video very well. A script that tells the learner how to perform a task without showing it won't be as effective as one that includes a demonstration. As the writer puts words on the page, he or she should be thinking all the time about what to show to help communicate with the learner. And more than just showing, what is moving? Video is a motion medium. Many tasks involve some kind of movement, and video can show that better than any other medium.

Later in the bread video, the script calls for the baker to test the dough as it is rising. She will press lightly on the dough to see whether it springs back. If it does not spring back, then the dough is finished rising. The words on the page don't communicate as well as seeing the action and seeing how the dough responds to a light touch. The writer visualized the motion and the close-up of the dough so the learner can actually see what to expect when the dough has finished rising. The video and script are on the CV4TT site.

All of this calls for some creativity on the part of the script writer. The creativity is in the service of learning, by making sure the script shows rather than tells and engages the learner in the content.

STYLE GUIDE

That creativity has certain boundaries to help the learner. We want to be sure that when we refer to the same object or concept we refer to it in a consistent way. For example, in the preceding section I referred to Mayer's Personalization Principle. Everywhere in this book when I refer to that principle I use exactly those words. I don't refer to personalization guidelines or rules. We want you to understand that I am referring to the same idea every time.

Those decisions about terminology, spelling, punctuation, and the like are reflected in a style guide. Small projects may not require a style guide. Large projects with large teams absolutely require them, so that everyone says things the same way.

If in one place one writer refers to a quiz, and in another place another writer calls the same thing a practice exercise, we may confuse the learner who expects that different terms mean different things.

Punctuation and spelling may be set out in an agreement that simply refers to a standard reference, such as a specific dictionary or grammar reference. Project-specific terms relate to the content, concepts, and interactions in a project.

In multimedia and video, the style guide will also include colors for specific purposes, terminology, and behavior of buttons and other controls, as well as page layouts and names for parts and subparts of the multimedia piece. The whole thing might be referred to as a course, which consists of modules, which in turn consist of topics. Other organizations might use terms like curriculum, strands, units, or levels.

There are style guides available that address specific needs. One used a lot for software training is the Microsoft style guide, which, as one might expect, defines a specific vocabulary for all of the objects in an interface for software. The *New York Times* and the Associated Press both publish style guides that work well for expository writing.

Even with a published style guide, each project will have its own vocabulary that all writers need to use consistently.

INTEGRATION WITH OTHER MEDIA

I have talked about the script in terms of the video, because that is the most demanding kind of script writing, dealing as it does with dialog, visual content, and specific shots.

Many teams use the same scripting format for the entire multimedia site, indicating where there is sound, what the visual content is, and sometimes what buttons or other objects are on the screen. This sort of detailed script has largely replaced the former storyboards that visually depict all parts of the site during scripting. Storyboards are still a part of feature film and game design.

Text that appears on screen will appear in the left column, while text in the right column will be recorded and played. In addition to text, the left column will describe graphics, animations, or other visual content. The right-hand column will include any notations on other sounds, such as sound effects or ambient sound.

In a small team, for small to medium projects, having one writer create all the content makes it easier to maintain consistent terminology and style throughout the project.

SCRIPT BREAKDOWN

Different members of the team have different needs for the script, and so the script will be broken down for each function.

One fundamental breakdown is a shot list. The team will want to break down the list by location, so that all the shots in one location can be done in the same session, if possible. Other considerations may include talent. Say there is an expert who is available to the team for a limited time. Any shots requiring the expert will have to be done in the time he or she is available.

Or there might be an expensive or hard-to-schedule prop or piece of equipment. I needed some video of a robot for a training video. The robot was in a training lab, but the lab was in use every day. To shoot the robot, we brought a crew in at night. We had to get all of the video we needed in one session and then return the robot to the configuration needed for the next day's class. A similar constraint will come up if your team needs to shoot in a retail location, such as might be needed for a corporate training module. They will not usually be able to shoot during business hours and will need to make best use of the overnight time they can schedule.

The camera operator and director (who might be the same person on a small team) need to know the order they'll be shooting in. In Chapter 10 on lighting we will see that each setup requires different lights. Using the sample script on Exhibit 4.1, once we get into the kitchen we have some medium shots (MS), close-ups (CU), and some extreme close-ups (ECU). Each of those is lit differently, so the team will want to be able to light for a series of shots, then tear down and light for another series of shots.

When breaking down the script to put it in shooting order, maintain the shot numbers from the original script, so that the editors can quickly find the required shots. They will be out of script order on the camera video, so those numbers are important. For that reason, I do not recommend using automatic paragraph numbering in your word processor when writing a script. Find where to turn it off and enter numbers manually. That way they won't change when you cut and paste the shots into a new order to create a shooting script.

In this script (a complete, slightly different version is on the CV4TT site), things get complicated pretty quickly, because they are working with a material, bread dough, that changes even while they are shooting. It will not work to order up a new batch of dough because, depending on how far they are into the shoot, it might take a couple of hours to get dough to the same stage.

We'll revisit scripts when we get to lighting and shooting. But for now, note that it's not unusual to have to go through the same sequence of actions several times to get all the shots we need for the final production. Go through once, leaving the camera rolling for a medium shot (or wider) as a cover for the whole action. Then shoot again for close-ups, with new lighting for each different close-up. In this script, with repeated close-ups of the interiors of mixing bowls, those can all be shot in the same setup. Since these are relatively small props, bring the bowl, whether a mixing bowl, the bowl for the stand mixer, or a small bowl for the melted butter, to the same location on the table and get the shots. Shoot the close-up of kneading in the same place, with minor adjustments to the lights.

Breaking down the script to show the exact sequence of shots is critical to make the best use of everyone's time and scarce resources. Your team may need a script breakdown to show which props are needed, which people, and which location for each scene. Some teams create a breakdown sheet for just such a purpose, listing all of those for each scene.

■ ■ ■

With the script breakdown complete, we have what we need to move to production. When we get to production, we'll talk about lights and lighting, sounds, and shooting. Before we start with that, we'll step back and look at other ways to produce video, all of which need the scripts produced in this chapter.

CHAPTER

5

OTHER WAYS TO PRODUCE VIDEO

So far, we have assumed that we're producing video in a traditional way, using a camera to record people or processes, then editing the resulting shots into a coherent video. A lot of video is produced in other ways.

When we want to create a video showing how to use a computer application, we don't point a camera at the monitor; we can use a screen recorder. A student has an idea for a fantasy video and creates thousands of single-frame images that she edits together into a story. A professor needs to explain an idea, or an activist wants to express an opinion and just talks into his webcam, recording the brief talk. A graphic artist uses Adobe Flash to create animations.

All of these demonstrate alternative ways of creating video. Some of these can fit within our workflow described in this book. Some do not and do not need to.

WEBCAMS

In the HBO series "Treme," Creighton Burnett, played by John Goodman, discovers YouTube and the ease with which he can record his angry post-Katrina rants using a webcam and share them with the world. (His daughter showed him the possibilities.)

Webcams may be external devices, connected to a computer with a USB cable, mostly used with desktop computers. Most laptops now include a webcam built into the bezel around the screen, which will also include a mic. Common brands are Logitech and Creative Labs, among many others.

Webcams were originally designed to facilitate video chats, with Skype or similar tools. A webcam can also be used to create acceptable, but limited, videos. It basically will record whatever it's pointed at, given that it's close enough to the webcam and well lit. The lenses in webcams are fairly wide-angle, since their basic purpose is to capture a human face just a couple of feet from the webcam itself. Some will allow the user to focus them; others are fixed focus. The software may allow face tracking, in which the image is centered on a face in the shot, even if the face moves. As with some other digital tricks, the webcam usually accomplishes that one by reducing resolution and picking the area of the shot that includes a face. A very few webcams track a face by turning the webcam within its mount, using small, quiet motors.

Using the software provided with the webcam or another tools, such as TechSmith Camtasia, the user sets up the webcam, checks the image to make sure the light is right, records a test, and then records the speech, diatribe (in the case of Creighton Burnett), or message.

The point of the test is to make sure the video looks and sounds right. If using the software that comes with the webcam, there is normally no choice of audio inputs. It will record what the mic in the webcam hears. With other software, there will normally be a choice of audio source, such as the mic in the external webcam, a mic built into the computer, mic connected to the Mic input, or a Bluetooth headset. As with all mics, a mic closer to the speaker will generally record better sound than one several feet away, as it is less likely to pick up background noises.

When recording with a webcam, look at the webcam, not the preview image on the screen, if you want to appear to be making eye contact with the viewer.

It is worth playing a little with the video captured by the webcam to see whether it is editable. There may be a choice of recording formats, and some may be better candidates for editing than others. One webcam I use offers a choice of .avi or .wmv files. Ordinarily, I would expect the .avi to be a better file for editing, but, since all .avi formats are not the same, I was unable to edit it in my usual video editing suite. The .wmv file worked well, though, so I simply changed the recording format to make sure I could edit. The .avi was editable in another suite, so it's worth experimenting to see what works.

Why would you want to edit a webcam video? I can think of a couple of reasons, some related to the way a webcam works and some related to the way I work.

When a webcam begins recording, it goes through a couple of seconds in which it adjusts for the lighting. That portion of the video is not something we want to publish. In recording, I generally wait a few seconds until the image on the screen looks good, then look down at the desktop, then up at the webcam and begin. I edit out the adjustment period, up to the point where I am looking down at the desktop. The video opens with me looking up at the webcam and beginning the talk. I get a smooth beginning, with none of the dark—then too light—then just-right as the webcam figures out what to do.

Sometimes I make a mistake in recording, or the cat walks into the shot, or my phone rings, or some other interruption. Rather than start over, I take care of the interruption and resume talking from some point prior to the interruption. Look for a place where there's a break in the talking, so you can cut there. When I edit, I remove all trace of the interruption and leave just the good parts.

The edited webcam video can be rendered in a variety of formats and distributed in any of the ways described in Chapter 22. The unedited video can be uploaded to YouTube and other video sharing sites and may be usable in a website without further work, depending on format.

SCREEN RECORDERS

When we want to demonstrate software or even record a PowerPoint presentation, screen recording software comes to the fore. Common brands are Adobe Captivate and TechSmith Camtasia. There are many others, some available at no cost.

Most screen recorders are integrated products, including the recording software, editor, and rendering engines.

The recording software offers a choice of recording a whole screen, a window, or a selectable region. Rarely do we need to record a whole screen, except when recording a presentation such as Microsoft PowerPoint, Apple Keynote, OpenOffice.org Impress, and other applications. The recorder may also offer the option of recoding a webcam image of the presenter. The recorder will capture the presentation and the presenter's voice. With a webcam, it will also capture the presenter's face.

At present it's arguable whether including a recording of the presenter's face is beneficial. Mayer's Personalization Principle suggests that learning is enhanced when there is a person associated with the instruction. An image or a recording would seem beneficial, in that light.

Mayer's Coherence Principle and Sweller's Cognitive Load Theory suggest minimizing extraneous content, including, it would seem, a recording of the presenter. It's a good research topic. At the time I'm writing, it might suit both to include an introductory presentation that includes a recording of the face of the presenter. Subsequent recordings could omit it. The introductory piece helps learners associate the voice and content with a real person, while the other recordings minimize distraction.

The screen capture programs are particularly valuable in demonstrating use of software. They will record the presenter's voice along with mouse movements, clicks, and other on-screen events. They can also record sounds from the software, if those are important. If the need is to show use of multiple applications, set the screen capture software to record a whole screen or a region. Then drag the applications into the recoding area or switch from one to the other. For example, I have demonstrated use of webpage editing software, then published a webpage to be viewed in a browser. The screen capture shows the steps in web editing, publishing, and then viewing in the browser, all in the same region of the screen. I control which is on top, and therefore what is recorded.

AFTER CAPTURE, YOU WILL WANT TO EDIT

The editors offer the capability of removing mistakes and other problem video, such as the startup of the webcam. In the editor, choose the placement of the image of the presenter, which may be to one side of the presentation or screen capture. Other capabilities common in the editor are placement of callouts, titles, or other text, highlighting areas of the screen, or using panning and zooming to view close-ups of the active area of the screen. The software follows the cursor to determine which areas of the screen to magnify. The editor may be able to correct color, remove some noise from sound recordings, and import still images or other features that enhance the video.

Some editors, specifically Adobe Captivate, allow other features, including pausing the play to allow the learner to respond to questions, click on buttons, and other actions that bring the notion of video closer to being a simulation in which the learner is actively responding rather than just watching.

The last step is to render the video, that is, produce the final, edited, enhanced video. There will be choices of formats, usually including Adobe Flash (.swf or .flv), Windows Media (.wmv) or .avi. There is more about video formats and distribution in Chapters 21 and 22.

The ability to render to an .avi file offers additional possibilities. The editors associated with the screen recorders are usually somewhat limited compared to dedicated editors such as Adobe Premiere, Apple Final Cut, and others. The standard .avi file produced by the screen recorder can then be further edited in another program, opening up capabilities for special effects, adding sound and music, using more elaborate titles, and intercutting video from other sources.

Screen recorders are special-purpose tools, but they fill an important place in our video production toolbox.

ADOBE FLASH ANIMATIONS

It is possible to develop videos with no camera at all. Adobe Flash and other animation programs give the more technical developer capabilities to create animations by drawing and animating them. Flash's "tween" function works particularly well in creating animations, since the artist need draw only the beginning and ending images. Flash fills in the frames in between.

That's cool, but with more technical ability, Flash can also be used to create interactive animations. A chemistry student can drag and drop lab apparatus to set up an experiment, without stepping out of her study room. A political science student can try what-if scenarios with Electoral College votes to see how various election strategies work, without spending a dime of campaign funds. Flash's scripting language allows creation of animations that use input from the student to interact with the content and change the animation on the fly. How to create these dynamic activities is well beyond the scope of this book, but I did want to raise the possibilities.

I refer to Flash because at present it offers capabilities for animations beyond other applications. That will surely change, especially with HTML5. Check the CV4TT website for updates.

SINGLE FRAME ANIMATIONS

In the early days of animated films, all animations were created by drawing on transparent materials, creating layers of cells that were then photographed, one frame at a time, to make a movie. Films run at twenty-four frames per second, so even a twelve-minute animated cartoon contains over 17,000 frames. This is very detailed, painstaking work. The upside is that anything that can be drawn is possible in an animation.

The basic approach is to shoot each frame with a digital still camera. The individual frames are then dropped into the video editor to make up the animated video. Rendering and distribution are in standard video formats. Since video runs at thirty frames per second, you'll need even more frames than our colleagues working with film.

The cell animation approach works, then, by creating the cells, photographing them, and bringing the still images into the video editor.

Another similar approach is to use a still camera to shoot images from a mini stage. One student created a stage from a shoebox, placing dollhouse-size furniture in it. The characters were made of modeling clay. She placed the characters on the stage, positioned them, and took several thousand still images. When a character needed to move, each frame showed the next part of the movement, such as getting up from a chair. All the intermediate positions needed to be posed. Say it takes a second to get up from a chair. That's thirty positions. Of course, it's possible to get smooth animation with fewer than thirty positions. Silent movies ran at eighteen frames per second. So she could get quite good animations by targeting fifteen frames per second as the effective rate, by inserting each still image twice, to produce one second, with fifteen different images, in sequence.

In edit, she added sound effects, video transitions, titles, and other effects to make a complete video.

That was an ambitious project, but simpler ones are certainly possible. Using drawn images or movable models of real items, animations are within the reach of a patient, careful teacher or trainer.

■ ■ ■

Most video starts with a camera. The options described in this chapter extend the range of the teacher or trainer with different techniques and tools. The screen recorder is probably the most common alternative tool, but the others have their places.

CHAPTER

6

MANAGING VIDEO PROJECTS

Video projects, even small ones, are complex undertakings. There are many more things to do than in other development projects, such as creating a website or an instructor's manual. More people are involved, even if only for a short time. Failure to plan has consequences. If you don't have the right video when you are ready to edit, there is not a lot you can do about it.

This chapter is not going to replace a good project management book or workshop. The Project Management Institute has a lot of good material on project management, mostly targeted to managing software projects. It is necessary to translate the examples to something that makes sense to instructional developers. In this chapter, I will attempt to hit the important highlights of project management as applied to instructional video projects.

COMPLEXITY

In smaller instructional development projects there is not much of a need for formal project management methodologies. Work is more or less linear, with few things going on at the same time. The penalties for mistakes aren't too serious. If you forgot to include some content in an instructor's guide, you can add it.

Video is not so forgiving. The same content goes through many transformations as you develop your project, as it goes from concept to script, to various breakdowns of the script, to video, then edit and final cut. These many transformations mean that it is not easy to go back and fix mistakes. Say you've left some important content out of the script. Your subject-matter expert doesn't notice the error until you get to edit. "Hey, we don't have anything about safety in this video. We really need to warn people about risks in this procedure." It is really hard at this point to add content for which you have no script and no video. If the team has limited access to the place where the video was shot, say in a remote plant or retail location, any solution at this point is at best going to be a workaround that will not have the quality of the rest of the production. Even in the best case, the project is going to be delayed.

Another source of complexity is the number of people involved in video production. While many of the activities can be completed by one person working alone, some cannot. The actual video shooting always requires extra people. In one simple video I shot, two scenes required a different location, in a church. I also needed an actor dressed as a priest, some props, and about a dozen extras, people not really characters in the video, but necessary to populate the scene. It was necessary to manage the project so I didn't waste the time of the people I asked to be there or disrupt the schedule of activities in the church. Only careful planning makes all of that work.

A final source of complexity is that there are a lot of steps necessary to complete a video project. Recall the description of the process in Chapter 2. There is a lot going on. We work to deadlines and budgets, and usually there is neither enough time nor money. Even small mistakes can cost both time and money or negatively impact the quality of our work. If we don't have enough time and money, poor planning just makes it worse. It's really important to get it right the first time.

This chapter will use project phases that map onto the ADDIE framework (analysis, design, development, implementation, and evaluation) but use project management terminology.

DEFINING THE PROJECT

In Chapter 3 on planning we dealt with parts of the first two project management activities, Defining the Project and Planning the Project. As we proceed, you'll see that planning gets far more detailed than we hinted at in the earlier chapter.

Defining the project includes setting goals and objectives, certainly, but with some added detail that we need in order to manage a project. Creating goals and objectives will require analyses of the tasks, content, audience, or context.

The objectives we talked about earlier were instructional or learning objectives. Here we're talking about project objectives, which deal with deliverables, quality, costs, and time. In order to create these objectives, we have to be much more specific about the project itself.

What is it that we are actually producing? It's all well and good as we conceptualize the project to talk about a multimedia website, with a couple of video segments, supported by text and graphics. We might even address the instructional strategies, story, and characters. In this phase we'll need to pull out our media specification (See

Chapter 2, One Time Through the Process) to get some definition about exactly what it is we are creating: How much video? How much text and graphics? What kinds of graphics? What kinds of interactions?

The team also needs to agree on when the project is due and what the budget is. This level of definition helps keep the project team together and, when agreed to by all parties, helps keep the scope within control.

It's worth saying at this point that you probably don't have really good estimates for these things. You will have to make some assumptions, based on any of these:

- Multimedia projects you've done before

- Multimedia you've seen and thought was close to what you want to do

- Best guesses based on how you've taught this content before

- Resources available for the project

The point of making assumptions is not just to have something to work from, but to acknowledge that these are best guesses. Then, as the project moves along, assumptions become specifications as the team learns and makes decisions about how to use resources and time.

In projects done for pay, it is common to provide budget and schedule estimates by phase. So when a project starts, it is possible to give firm estimates for analysis and design and rough estimates for development and subsequent phases. Then when design is complete, with better understanding of exactly what will be needed in the project, it's possible to come up with very solid estimates of development costs and time.

PLANNING

Note: There is a project management file on the CV4TT website called MultimediaSampleProject.xml. I created the file using the free Open Project software from Capterra, but you can use Microsoft Project to open it if you have it. Or download Open Project if you don't.

The planning phase of project management requires quite a bit of work to do well. Some people avoid detailed planning because it is a lot of work and they mistakenly think they can somehow make up for lack of planning by exerting extra effort when problems occur. The consequence of not planning is much more work (and pain) later in the project as the consequences of poor planning make themselves known.

There are three principal aspects to planning: the work breakdown structure (WBS), roles, and resources. Of these, the WBS is what most people find most difficult.

TASKS/ACTIVITIES

A key part of project planning is figuring out what the team has to do to complete the project. In project management language, Activities are the deliverables (tangible things) the project has to create. They are listed as nouns in the WBS because they are things. Tasks are the thing people do to create the deliverables. They are phrased as verbs. For example, Figure 6.1 lists the Content Outline as an Activity. It is something the team needs to create. Below that (and indented in this software) are three tasks that someone on the team has to do to create a Content Outline.

Experienced project managers can sit down with their project management software and enter the activities and tasks. Those with less experience can approach it in another way.

One way is top-down. List the activities and then list the activities and tasks that need to be done to create the deliverable listed in the activity. Yes, an activity can contain another activity. Say we're doing a very large multimedia project, with three separate modules. Each module could be listed as an activity. Then we would have activities within that, such as Storyboard, Script, Video Shoot, and so forth, for each module. The Script activity would then be broken down into tasks, such as write first draft, review, and revise.

Another approach, probably easier for new project managers, is to go bottom-up. Start listing all the things your team needs to do to create the project. Don't worry at this point about phrasing, order, hierarchy, redundancy, or anything but listing everything you can think of.

Brainstorming is one way to do this activity. Write all the ideas on individual sticky notes. Once your team has run out of ideas, start moving notes around to organize them, in an outline form.

The draft-review-revise sequence in Figure 6.1 is really common and will occur throughout the WBS. Not everything lends itself to that, such as the Video Shoot activity. It has other tasks that the team needs to account for. Creating the web pages will have other tasks as well, such as loading them on a development server and testing. Details are shown in Figure 6.2.

As we enter activities and tasks, we can also enter durations, that is, how long it will take to do something. Enter durations only for tasks, not activities. If your project management plan is set up correctly, the software will roll up tasks into activities, no matter how deeply nested.

Estimating duration is not easy. Most people tend to be somewhat optimistic about estimating time. That is one reason many people are late to meetings: They underestimated the time needed to get there. The first time you do a video project, you have

⊟ Content Outline	2 days	7/1
Draft content outline	1 day	7/1
Review content outline	0.5 days	7/5
Revise content outline	0.5 days	7/5

FIGURE 6.1. *Part of Work Breakdown Structure.*

⊟ **Video shoot**	**4 days**	**7/1**
Visit site	1 day	7/1
Block	0.062 days	7/1
Plan shots	2 days	7/1
Plan lighting	2 days	7/1
Walkthrough	1 day	7/1
Live rehearsal	1 day	7/1
Shoot	2 days	7/1

FIGURE 6.2. *Detail of the Shooting Activity.*

little empirical basis for estimating your time. As you gain experience, your estimates get better.

Even for the new manager, there are things to do to help improve the time estimates. One is to estimate smaller tasks, that is, break the tasks down more finely. Small tasks are easier to estimate than large ones. I pretty well know how long it takes to walk a mile. I have little clue how long it takes to walk from my home in Detroit to San Francisco.

Another is to bias the estimate of time. A classic formula is

$$T_E = \frac{T_o + 4T_L + T_P}{6}$$

Where T_E is the estimated time, T_O is the optimistic time estimate, T_L is the most likely estimate, and T_P is a pessimistic estimate. Because there are six estimates (we weight the likely estimate by 4), we take an average by dividing by 6 to get the final estimate T_E.

Let's do an example, based on my driving time to work. My optimistic estimate is fifteen minutes. My most likely time is twenty-two minutes. A pessimistic estimate is sixty minutes, if the weather is bad, there's an accident on the freeway, or some other problem or combination of problems. That gives me an expression like this:

$$T_E = \frac{15 + 4 * 22 + 60}{6}$$

And this calculates out to 27.167 minutes (that's 27 minutes, 10 seconds, in the usual way of saying things), or, for our purposes, twenty-seven minutes. That's the estimate I would use. It turns out to be pretty good.

But it won't always be twenty-seven minutes. It turns out that about 85 percent of the time it will be twenty-seven minutes or less. That's pretty good. But about 15 percent of the time it will be longer, maybe as much as an hour. Won't that mess up my schedule? Yes, it will. But remember this is not the only task we need to estimate. We'll have dozens to hundreds of tasks. Some will turn out longer than estimates, some will be right on target, some will come out in less time. On average, we'll be OK. And our schedule will be OK, in total.

Now I must say I don't actually do the calculation I just showed you. What I do is bias the estimate I get from people on the team to accommodate their optimism. If someone tells me editing the video will take three days, I may put four in the schedule. That incorporates the tug on the schedule that the pessimistic estimate brings. Or if my experience with this editor is that she really underestimates the time, I may go with five days.

Where do the estimates come from? The best way is to obtain them from the team, from the people who will have to do the work. The basic practical reason for using their estimates is they are the people who have to live with the times they give. If the project manager hands out a schedule with estimated times for the team, without consulting them, they have no buy-in to the schedule. But if the numbers are theirs, or at least they had a part in coming up with the numbers, then they have an interest in making the schedule work.

Your software probably now lists the same start date for all tasks and activities. Do not be tempted to enter dates for these. Let the software do the heavy lifting. We will use the Predecessors (sometimes called dependencies) to establish sequence and set estimated dates for everything but the start of the project. The start date needs to be set manually.

Some tasks need to be done before others. The draft script needs to be completed before the editor can begin. In project management language, that means the task, Draft the Script, is a predecessor to Edit the Script. The software has a place to enter predecessor tasks, identified by the number in the left column. Figure out these dependencies, noting that the sequence they were entered in does not determine dependencies. For example, in the sample plan on the CV4TT website, the activity HTML pages can be done in parallel with all the activities and tasks related to creating the video. So the predecessor for the first task in HTML pages is the Storyboard, shown by listing the last completed task in the Storyboard activity.

Establishing these dependencies is key to letting the project management software do the hard work. If a project manager takes the obvious (and easy to do up-front) approach of entering actual dates rather than dependencies, problems multiply as the project gets underway. When tasks are completed, the manager will replace estimated dates with actual dates. Using predecessors, the software will calculate the new estimated dates, based on the actual. If the manager has entered the dates manually, she or he will have to enter the new dates rather than let the software calculate them. It's much more work later. This is another example of the idea of trading a little pain up-front for a lot of pain later.

How detailed does your WBS need to be? There are some general guidelines to help. If your WBS is too finely detailed, the project manager will go crazy keeping it up-to-date and will probably abandon the effort. If it's too coarse, the schedule won't be useful.

The longest tasks should be of three to five days' duration. Some will be a lot shorter and a very few will be longer. Shorter tasks become hard to keep track of. Longer tasks present a different problem. Say the project is eight weeks long in total, but your schedule lumps together all the website development into one task that's three weeks long. That means if the website development is taking too long, it might be three weeks before the project manager is aware there is a serious problem. That's nearly half the project duration. By the time the task is late, too much time has gone by to recover by rescheduling, assigning more resources, or slimming down the task.

All tasks should have a clear start and end event. That is, it should be clear from the predecessor what needs to be in place before the task can begin. And the task should have a defined deliverable, that is, a product, so the team knows when a task is done.

NOTE

The astute reader will see right away that "team meeting" is not a task under this definition. A meeting as such does not have a clear deliverable. "Come to consensus on site design" does have a deliverable, although the consensus might come about through a team meeting. Make sure meetings have a purpose and a result.

With these guidelines, the project manager will be able to build a useful WBS that is not burdensome to actually execute.

ROLES

An essential part of project planning is figuring out the roles needed to complete a project. The team will almost certainly require these roles:

- Instructional designer
- Project manager
- Videographer
- Writer
- Graphic artist
- Subject-matter expert
- Web developer

- Video editor

- Sound designer

- Editor

- Lighting director

These are not necessarily all different people. On video projects run by teachers and trainers, people will take on multiple roles. Some roles should be filled by different people. The writer and editor should be different people. A writer cannot edit his or her own work. The instructional designer and subject-matter expert should be different people. It is not uncommon for SMEs to include a lot of nice-to-know information that lengthens a program (and takes more time and effort to include) without improving the actual product or the learner's knowledge and performance at the end of the program. An instructional designer will challenge content recommendations to make sure the project doesn't include anything that doesn't need to be there.

Some roles overlap well. The same person might be instructional designer, writer, and project manager, although that person will have a lot to do, particularly at the beginning of the project. A graphic artist might also serve as lighting director and videographer, perhaps even web developer.

RESOURCES

Resources include people, equipment, space, or anything else needed to complete a project. Project managers need to make sure the team has the resources they need.

Most often, project managers concern themselves scheduling people's time and effort. As just noted, people and roles are overlapping concepts. After creating the work breakdown structure, setting predecessors, and estimating task durations, assign people (that is, resources) to each task. Do not assign people to activities, only to tasks.

Most project management software is set up to allow the project manager to define resources and then assign them to tasks. Part of the definition is setting how much time the resource is available to the project. This step is important because in this kind of project, people usually are not available full-time. If the designer is only available 50 percent of full-time, the schedule will reflect that a three-day task might take the designer more than one calendar week to complete it.

ADJUSTING THE SCHEDULE

The work breakdown structure is complete, durations have been entered, resources defined and assigned, and the project schedule shows a completion date three weeks beyond the deadline. After acknowledging that it's better to know that now rather than reach the deadline without having everything done, this is a common problem.

The manager can't just go through and adjust all the task durations downward. Assuming the estimates are honest, that sort of cheating to get the schedule to work causes pain at the end of the project. The manager does need to go through the tasks and check the durations to see whether any can be reduced. This refinement is best done with those responsible for completing the tasks. It's a negotiation process.

What else can the manager do? One key step is to check the predecessors to make sure they are accurate. Does everything need to be as sequential as the schedule is laid out? Are there tasks that can be done in parallel, saving calendar time?

Sometimes it will help to break a large task into smaller ones, allowing some parallel processing. Say we've scheduled all of the script as one writing task. It's followed by an edit task, reviews, and revision. The edit and review steps do not involve the writer.

We can reduce the calendar time by dividing the writing task into a couple of parts, perhaps by module, topic, or some other breakdown. Then, editing and reviewing can proceed while the writer goes on to the next part of the script.

In the sample WBS shown in Figure 6.3, there are two ways to schedule the same work. In the upper schedule, starting with Task 2, the script is treated as one task, with editing, reviewing and revising strung out afterward, in sequence. The second WBS, starting with Task 6, takes advantage of breaking the script down into three smaller parts.

		Name	Duration	Start	Finish
1		start of work	0 days	2/25/11 8:00 AM	2/25/11 8:00 AM
2		Write script	9 days	2/25/11 8:00 AM	3/9/11 5:00 PM
3		edit script	3 days	3/10/11 8:00 AM	3/14/11 5:00 PM
4		review script	1.5 days	3/15/11 8:00 AM	3/16/11 1:00 PM
5		revise script	3 days	3/16/11 1:00 PM	3/21/11 1:00 PM
6		Write part 1	3 days	2/25/11 8:00 AM	3/1/11 5:00 PM
7		edit part 1	1 day	3/2/11 8:00 AM	3/2/11 5:00 PM
8		review part 1	0.5 days	3/3/11 8:00 AM	3/3/11 1:00 PM
9		revise part 1	1 day	3/7/11 8:00 AM	3/7/11 5:00 PM
10		Write part 2	3 days	3/2/11 8:00 AM	3/4/11 5:00 PM
11		edit part 2	1 day	3/7/11 8:00 AM	3/7/11 5:00 PM
12		review part 2	0.5 days	3/8/11 8:00 AM	3/8/11 1:00 PM
13		revise part 2	1 day	3/8/11 1:00 PM	3/9/11 1:00 PM
14		Write part 3	3 days	3/9/11 1:00 PM	3/14/11 1:00 PM
15		edit part 3	1 day	3/14/11 1:00 PM	3/15/11 1:00 PM
16		review part 3	0.5 days	3/15/11 1:00 PM	3/15/11 5:00 PM
17		revise part 3	1 day	3/16/11 8:00 AM	3/16/11 5:00 PM

FIGURE 6.3. *Parallel Processes Shorten Overall Time, Without Adding to Effort or Resources.*

The second WBS allows each resource the same time to do the work, but it's scheduled so work can go on in parallel and it finishes five calendar days, or three business days, earlier. It's this kind of fine-tuning that can dramatically improve a schedule.

If reworking durations and the work breakdown structure still leave the schedule too long, the project may be too ambitious for the time and resources allowed. Here are some choices:

- *Reduce the scope*. Figure out what you absolutely have to include and cut out the rest. Reduce the amount of video and rely more on still images, text, and sound. Maybe it's possible to deliver a slimmed-down version by the deadline and later enhance it.

- *Find more resources*. An extra person or two, even for a short period, may bring the schedule back in line. Look for tasks that don't require detailed knowledge of the project so the team doesn't lose a lot of time bringing a new person up to speed.

- *Negotiate a later deadline*. Have the project completed for next semester or the next round of training rather than the immediate one. This alternative is probably the least satisfactory. Usually, if the project is needed, it's needed right away. Delaying it may mean the project really isn't necessary to do.

With the plan completed, it's time to begin work.

EXECUTING

Getting the work done requires different management skills than planning the project. Much of the planning work is done by the project manager, working alone. The execution is a team effort. The project manager gets work done through other people, so the task really becomes more leading than managing.

The project manager is concerned now with meeting budget, schedule, content, and quality targets. These four targets are interrelated, of course. A project that takes longer to complete will also cost more. When increasing budget or time is not possible, content may have to be reduced, which affects quality. When people feel rushed to get work done, quality may suffer.

MONITORING

Budget and schedule are the easiest. As tasks are completed, enter the actual dates into the project management software and watch what happens to the end date. Some tasks, if they are late, will push the end date out. Others make no difference. The project manager needs to know which are which. The project management software will calculate the critical path, which identifies which tasks must be completed on time to meet the deadline. Others are not critical and the software will calculate the slack, that is, how much the task could be delayed without consequences to the overall schedule.

Knowing which tasks are critical helps the project manager adjust resources and schedules while the project is in execution phase, moving resources to critical tasks that are running late while letting non-critical ones slide.

It all sounds so mechanical: "adjusting resources" sounds like turning knobs on a control panel. Remember that resources are people. As a project manager, adjusting resources means asking people to do something other than what they were expecting to do: "Stop working on that Module 2 script for now and help Fred with the Module 1 editing." This is where leadership comes in. The team members need to be invested in the success of the project so that inconveniences like being asked to change tasks are seen as worthwhile. The project manager sets the example by being willing to do whatever he or she asks someone else to do. If the team needs to stay late to make a deadline, the project manager needs to be there, working alongside.

Monitoring quality is also a key part of project management. To some project managers, it is the most important part of the job. It's a matter of perspective. After a year, memories of being late or over budget will fade. But as long as the video project is in use, lapses in quality will be evident.

The team should have an agreement on what is meant by quality. For the kinds of projects we're talking about in this book, there isn't always a customer for the product. If there is a customer, such as an administrator or committee, they define quality. That is, the person or group that is paying for it decides what the expectations are.

But most often there is not a clear customer. The team's shared vision for the project defines quality. What is good enough? What needs to be redone?

NOTE

Don't shy away from "good enough." However well you have done your work, there is always room for improvement. The desire for perfection, however defined, has put more projects behind schedule and over budget than any other malady. Perfect is the enemy of done.

If a project slips behind schedule or is going over budget, the project manager and team have the same choices as we saw earlier in project planning: adjust resources, adjust time, or adjust content.

None of this management works without tracking and monitoring. I have seen projects in large corporations where the project manager printed the Gantt chart (like those in Figure 6.3) and pasted it on the wall. It was very impressive, many sheets of paper, covering the wall of the conference room that they called the "War Room."

But after a couple of weeks it was useless. The printed version was out-of-date as soon as the project started, because some tasks were done early, others were late, a few were on time. The whole schedule shifts and twists as real dates and costs replace estimates.

The software allows the manager to take snapshots at various times through the project, to track slippage and changes. The first of these sets a baseline. Then the manager can compare whatever the schedule currently shows to the baseline. The comparison tells the project manager what needs attention and where there are potential problems.

REPORTING AND CONTROLLING

If there is a customer, a critical part of execution is keeping the customer in the loop. Regular status meetings include reports with these headings:

- What was planned for the last reporting period

- What was completed in the last reporting period

- What is planned for the next reporting period

- Problems encountered, along with strategies to mitigate the problems

- What the team needs from the customer

Following the status meetings, or any meeting with the customer, the project manager sends a memo to all parties summarizing any decisions made at the meeting and listing action items and unresolved issues.

Even in projects for which there isn't a clear customer, these status reports and memos are helpful for the team. Some project management software allows web reports that make schedules available to anyone on the team all the time.

Customers occasionally ask for revisions or changes that were not in the original plan. They don't do it because they're trying to get more than was agreed to. In fact, in my experience it's usually a misunderstanding. The regular status meetings and follow-up memos are the record of decisions and can usually resolve disagreements over what was promised.

When there is a real change to content, then the project manager and the team revise the schedule and budget to accommodate the changes.

DELIVERING AND CLOSING

It's done. The last edits are completed, the project has been rendered to final form and integrated into a website. It's been tested for both technical function and instructional benefit. It's been launched in the production environment. Smiles and congratulations all around! Maybe the project manager will pop for extra donuts to celebrate.

From a project management view, there are still some things to do. It's not a long list, but it's critical to updating this project and to later projects that these things be done right, while memories are fresh. Document the project and learn from it.

Conduct a lessons learned session. With the whole team participating, list things gone wrong and things gone right. Without placing blame, why did some things go wrong? What will you do next time to head off the problem? What went well? What should the team do in the next project to make sure they haven't lost what they did and how and why they did it that way.

Likely everyone will want to take credit for things gone right. There will also likely be some defensiveness with things gone wrong. It's important for the team to understand that they are trying to make sure it doesn't happen again, so a clear understanding of what happened and why is necessary. It's not sufficient to say that someone messed up. It's rare that one person's mistake causes a major problem for a project. Other actions, processes, or tools contributed to it or permitted the mistake to have the impact it did.

Assume that everyone acted with the best of intentions, based on the information he or she had at the time.

The relevant questions focus on the process, tools, and information people had. Once the emphasis is off from specific individuals, the team can understand and prevent future problems.

Documenting the process means making a record of decisions and deliverables. The team cannot wait until closing the project to begin documentation, but closing is a key event for documentation.

The memos the project manager produced after status meeting, prototypes, all deliverables, source code for programming (if any), raw and edited video files, scripts, and other documents need to be archived so they can be found again. Many projects need some updating later. Having the archive available makes updating much easier. The documentation can also be used as samples for later projects.

■ ■ ■

This chapter ends Section I of *Creating Video for Teachers and Trainers*. We've talked through why we want to consider video, planning, and managing the project. In Section II, we become much more specific to your projects. We look at the equipment we'll need to make our video.

CHAPTER

YOUR ASSIGNMENT 1

Plan and write a script for a short video, approximately two or three minutes long (300 to 450 words of dialog).

Plan

- Describe the content and audience.

- State the purpose.
    - If the video script is part of a larger production, for example, a website, state the specific purpose of the video, but also describe how it fits the larger context.

- Design Considerations: First Principles, Problems
    - What is the problem your learners need to solve? What instruction do they need to solve the problem?

- Story and Character
    - What's the story? What characters will you need for your script?

Script

- Write a script in two-column A/V format that is consistent with the plan described above.

Instructors: It may help to make this two separate assignments, with the plan due before the script. Allow time to review and return the plan before the script is due.

SECTION

II

ESSENTIAL EQUIPMENT

CHAPTER

8

CAMCORDERS

Selecting a camcorder for your production can be confusing because of the wide range of choices. Let's walk through the choices to help you decide what to buy or rent for your production.

NOTE

Rent? Yes, many producers rent equipment simply because it is costly to buy when technology changes rapidly. For most readers of this book, buying is probably the best choice because we're looking at relatively inexpensive equipment. Rental will give you much better equipment, but probably at a price that would permit you to buy a consumer-grade camcorder. When buying, you will have to assume that you'll replace a camcorder on a regular basis, especially if you are shooting a lot of video. Consumer gear is meant for occasional use. The camcorders used by my students typically last no more than three years.

VIDEO FORMATS

Your first choice is whether you want to be able to shoot high definition video (HD) or standard definition (SD). HD can be downgraded to SD in post-production, but you cannot upgrade from SD to HD. For video that you intend to use on the web, with relatively small images, SD is adequate. If you want to be able to run web video at full screen, you'll want HD video.

High def video is recorded with more data than SD video. SD video, a standard since the beginning days of television, records 525 lines of video, writing fields of alternate lines sixty times a second (interlaced video) so that you get a complete image thirty times a second. The screen is 3x4 aspect ratio, meaning it is 1 1/3 (4/3) times as wide as it is high.

HD video writes 720 or 1080 lines, either interlaced or progressive (every line is written in sequence). There are then four combinations possible: 720i, 720p, 1080i, and 1080p. In general, 1080 will give better images than 720, and progressive scan gives a better image than interlaced scan. An HD video image has an aspect ratio of 9x16, meaning it is 16/9 times as wide as it is high. This is a significantly wider image than SD and looks more like feature film. Stats are shown in the chart below and illustrated in Figure 8.1.

	Standard Definition	**High Definition**
Resolution	525 lines, interlaced	720 or 1080 lines, interlaced or progressive
Aspect ratio	3x4	9x16

You may think the choice of video format has price consequences, and all other things being equal, you'd be right. But all other things are rarely equal. In consumer-grade equipment, to acquire features that you need, you may only have choices that

3 × 4
Standard video

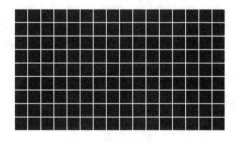

9 × 16
HD video

FIGURE 8.1. *3x4 and 9x16 rectangles.*

are HD. That happens because some of the things we require only are found on more expensive camcorders.

Let's look at those other features.

LENS

Consumer grade camcorders do not offer a choice of lens. When you select a model, there is only one lens for that model. We do need to consider the lens to make sure the model will work for you.

All come with zoom lenses. That is, these lenses have variable focal length. Focal length determines the field of view of a lens, whether wide (short focal length) or narrow (long focal length). Narrow field of view is usually called telephoto. With a zoom, you can change the field of view by adjusting the lens. Note that on these camcorders, the zoom control is electronic, meaning you press a button or rocker switch and small motors move the internal parts of the lens to adjust the focal length. The electronic control does not provide the fine control that professional zooms do, with their manual adjustments. It is sometimes difficult to get a slow, controlled zoom with the electronic controls. For that reason, I avoid zooming while shooting. It's sometimes necessary, of course. See Figure 8.2 for a comparison of field of view for wide angle and telephoto settings.

Lenses vary in quality and in the available focal lengths. On good name-brand camcorders, the lenses are quite good through the middle of the focal length range. At the extremes, you may encounter some defects. In particular, at the widest setting, you may encounter some vignetting, meaning the corners of the image are either not as sharply in focus or may be darker because less light is available at the edges. (Figure 8.4 shows an example.) Some distortion, known as pincushion distortion (Figure 8.3), may be evident at the widest setting, in which parallel lines appear to curve away from each other at the center of the shot.

Normal lens   Telephoto lens   Wide lens
                        (long)   (short)

FIGURE 8.2. *Field of View.*

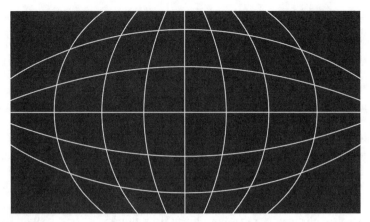

FIGURE 8.3. *Pincushion.*

FIGURE 8.4. *Vignetting.*

Another problem with zoom lenses may be that the zoom range is not as useful as you'd like. Wide lenses (short focal length) are fairly large in diameter, so to save money, lens makers may sacrifice the wide end of the zoom range. You may find that the widest setting is still too narrow for comfortable use inside a home or small office. Camcorder makers will often tell you the 35mm equivalent focal length, which makes an easy comparison from one camcorder to another. The widest (smallest number) should be at least 35mm, meaning that a 10x zoom would have a range of 35 to 350 mm, which is quite a useful range.

NOTE

Why not just use the actual focal length, instead of 35mm equivalent?

The actual focal length of the lens does not tell you how wide the field of view is, without also knowing the dimensions of the charge coupled device (CCD) chip that gathers the light. Then you'd need a table or do some calculations to compare camcorders if the chips are not the same size. By using a standard comparison (35mm film), camcorder makers help you compare unequal lenses.

For reference, a "normal" field of view on a 35mm camera is a 50 or 55mm lens. A 30mm lens is a wide angle, and a 20mm is a fisheye (very wide angle). A 105mm lens is a medium telephoto, good for portraits and close-ups. At 200mm or 300mm, we're into long telephoto. At these settings, camera shake is noticeable and a tripod is essential.

Zoom lenses are advertised as having some ratio of longest to widest settings, such as 10x or 20x, meaning the longest focal length is ten or twenty times the shortest. They may quote ratios as high as 200x, in which case they're counting two kinds of zoom, optical and digital. Optical zoom is that available from manipulating the lens elements. The image size remains unchanged and the quality is nearly uniform throughout the range of a well-designed lens.

Digital zooms are far less useful. In fact, I advise my students to turn off the digital zoom except in cases of life or death. The digital zoom narrows the field of view by using successively smaller areas of the chip sensor, expanding the pixels to cover the original image size. Even at the tightest (longest) optical zoom setting, the image covers the entire chip surface. To effectively double the focal length digitally, the camera electronically limits the image to just the center portion of the chip. (The diagonal of the reduced area will be half that of the full chip.) It then processes the image by doubling each pixel to regain the original size.

Say the chip resolution is 1024x768. That's about 786,000 pixels. By using digital zoom to "double" the effective focal length, we reduce the numbers of pixels actually used in the image to the center 196,500. Then the camcorder pulls those back out to 1024x768 by enlarging each pixel, resulting in an image that is no longer very sharp, and at higher zooms actually looks very blocky ("pixellated") because the pixels are enlarged so much (actually four times in this example).

SENSORS

We've mentioned the sensor a couple of times. So let's see what this actually is. The sensor, usually one CCD (charge coupled device), is a light sensitive electronic device that manipulates a small electrical current to represent the light falling on the photosensitive area. This electrical current is then converted to a digital signal that the camcorder can record.

There are several important characteristics to be considered. One is simply the number of CCD chips in the camcorder. Most consumer camcorders make do with one chip that captures all the colors. Using one chip saves money, weight, and complexity compared to professional 3CCD camcorders. In those professional camcorders, prisms separate the light into its component red, green, and blue primary colors, sending each to its own dedicated chip. The electronics then process the colors for recording.

RESOLUTION AND SIZE

It's usually easy to compare resolutions of several camcorders. It will be stated as .786 megapixels or 1024x768, or comparable numbers. Because of the ease of comparison, manufacturers often tout the resolution as though it were the most important factor.

But a small chip with high resolution results in very small pixels that may not be able to gather enough light to make a good image. So chip size also matters. Unfortunately, for obscure reasons rooted in the distant past, sensor sizes are not reported in a clear manner. For example, one Canon camcorder specification reports a sensor size of 1/2.6″. Another is 1/6″. These are fractions, even with the curious 2.6 as a denominator. The first one (1/2.6″) is larger than 1/6″. To check this you could actually do the calculation to make the numbers comparable. The larger one is about 0.38 square inches. The smaller one is about 0.17 square inches. Big difference. The larger one will gather much more light and produce a better image, all other things being equal.

Higher megapixel count with a larger sensor will result in a better image.

STORAGE MEDIA

In the recent past, tape was the standard storage medium. It is reliable, inexpensive, and long-lasting. It was normal practice for videographers to never reuse a tape, because storing tapes allowed keeping a lot of video in a small space.

But tapes depend on a finicky transport mechanism inside the camcorder that has to be kept scrupulously clean and is easily damaged by the rough handling common on location shoots. A metal recording head spins against the tape surface to record or play the video, slightly damaging the tape each time it is used. The magnetic coating rubs off on the head, requiring regular cleaning.

Solid state chips (SD chips or flash drives) depend on no mechanical devices and are extremely rugged. They are small and very reliable. They cost more than tapes but do not degrade with each use, making reuse a reasonable proposition. For these reasons, chips and flash memory are now the media of choice in consumer grade camcorders.

Professional camcorders continue to use tape (usually MiniDV format) or hard disk drives (HDD) for storage.

NECESSARY FEATURES

Since you are not just shooting family events, for which viewers have a pretty high tolerance for technical problems, there are some features you need on a camcorder that may drive you toward more expensive choices than what you would need just for informal shooting.

You want to attach an external microphone or mic (pronounced mīc, rhymes with like). The on-board mic in the camcorder is not adequate to capture good sound. It is too close to the operator and too far from the talent. With low-end camcorders, which often have no mic input jack, you are limited to what the built-in mic can capture.

The mic input on consumer camcorders is usually a mini jack (1/8″ or 3.5 mm) color coded red.

You want to be able to use manual controls for white balance, exposure, and focus. The automatic controls work well much of the time. But in some circumstances, such as a strong backlight or outdoor shooting in the snow or on a white beach, the automatic exposure will leave your subject in the dark. Look for a camcorder that has the option of manual control.

You need a tripod socket on the bottom of the camcorder, since you cannot hold the camcorder steady enough to make professional quality video. But for the occasions when you need to handhold, you must have a viewfinder. The flip-out LCD panel forces you to hold the camcorder out in front of your body, making for an unstable shooting platform. The viewfinder allows you to use two hands and brace the camcorder against your head to get a stable, mostly jitter-free shot, as long as you stay at wider zoom settings.

You'll need a headphone jack on the camcorder, usually labeled with an image of headphones. This jack allows you to monitor the sound as you shoot, to make sure you are getting the sound you want, with a minimum of background noise. The jack may be shared with the A/V Out (see below) or may be its own, color coded black.

It helps to be able to buy larger capacity batteries so you can shoot for longer periods of time without worrying about power.

Finally, it helps to have an output jack on the camcorder that allows you to plug in a monitor so others can see what you're shooting. The subject-matter expert or designer will want to see as you shoot. The jack may be labeled A/V Out and is often yellow. Other suitable options are S-video and HDMI. High-definition camcorders will usually have HDMI, which will connect to a high-def monitor or TV set.

It is helpful to buy a camcorder from a physical store. You can see and hold it to make sure it's comfortable. You can see whether the arrangement of controls and jacks will work for you. Over time you'll develop some preferences that may be clearer when you hold the camcorder rather than view it on a website. I like controls that are physical buttons rather than touch screen spots. The touch screen spots can be difficult to see when shooting outdoors, especially when smudged. Others may not agree, but you won't know until you try it.

There are many websites that do detailed reviews of camcorders. I am more comfortable with expert reviewers than crowd-sourced anonymous users. While I may learn something from those casual reviews, I appreciate the rigor of professional reviewers, who are more likely to use the equipment in the same demanding ways that we will use it.

■ ■ ■

Your camcorder is the most important piece of equipment. Select carefully, knowing there is no ideal device; then use it and take good care of it. We'll learn about how to use it in the next chapter.

CHAPTER

USING THE CAMCORDER

In this chapter we'll discuss basic visual composition, shots, and camera movement. The viewer may not be able to tell you how to improve the shots in your video, but will gain an overall impression of the quality from how you compose your shots and, in general, use the camcorder.

COMPOSITION

The center of the frame is a weak spot for the center of attention. That is, it's an uninteresting, uninspired spot in the frame. Look at the images that make a lasting impression on you, like the Mona Lisa. Her eyes draw your attention, and they are not at the center of the image. Her face is roughly a third of the way down from the top.

This image, and many others, suggest a rule of thirds. Figure 9.1 is an example.

While the Mona Lisa is centered left to right, the composition uses thirds vertically. The camera operator will compose shots so that eyes or other important content are placed above center or, less often, off-center to the left or right.

When shooting a person who is moving or looking to one side, out of the frame, allow extra space on the side the person is moving or looking toward.

This use of "nose space" enhances the sense of motion and feels less crowded to the viewer (Figure 9.2).

FIGURE 9.1. *Rule of Thirds.*

FIGURE 9.2. *Photo Showing Nose Space.*

COMMON SHOTS

You will often shoot individuals or small groups of people. There are some common shots that you will use and see called for in scripts. Let's start with shots of an individual.

FIGURE 9.3. *Medium Shot.*

FIGURE 9.4. *Bust shot.*

A *medium* or *waist* shot places the shot so that the person's waist is at the bottom of the frame. The face will be about one-third of the way down from the top. (See Figure 9.3.)

A *bust* or *close-up* places the talent's chest at the bottom of the shot. The eyes will be at the top third. (See Figure 9.4.)

FIGURE 9.5. *Extreme Close-Up.*

FIGURE 9.6. *2-Shot, Medium.*

An extreme close-up (Figure 9.5) fills the frame with the talent's face. This shot can be uncomfortable for the viewer, since we are not accustomed to being this close to another person. For that reason it can be effective in showing emotion, introspection, or reflection, if not overused.

FIGURE 9.7. *3-Shot, Wide.*

FIGURE 9.8. *Over-the-Shoulder (OTS) Shot.*

Other shots show more than one person. So we have a *2-shot* or, less often, a *3-shot*. Because we're showing more than one person, these are usually medium shots or wide shots, as in Figures 9.6 and 9.7.

One 2-shot is so commonly used it has its own name, the over-the-shoulder or OTS shot. This shot is often used in pairs, in dialogs or interviews. One shot shows

FIGURE 9.9. *Pair of OTS Shots.*

FIGURE 9.10. *Dialog Set with Line.*

FIGURE 9.11. *False Reverse of Dialog Above.*

one person's face, and the other shot shows the other's. Figures 9.8 and 9.9 illustrate these shots.

There is one important caution to observe. Imagine that there is a line through the two people in the dialog and extending beyond them as seen in Figure 9.10.

Do not cross the line in moving the camera for the second OTS shot. The viewer will see the people reversed left to right, as in Figure 9.11. This error is known as a *false reverse.* It is often invisible to those on the shoot, because their mental images place the talent as they were on the shoot. Other viewers, without that mental image, will perceive that the people have traded positions.

CAMERA MOVEMENT

The camera may move in two ways. It can move by changing its position on the tripod. It can also move by you physically moving the tripod itself, although with our equipment, these moves are somewhat difficult.

One common movement is a "pan," short for panoramic. The camera pivots horizontally on the tripod, moving from left to right or right to left. The best use of a pan is to follow action or movement of the talent. Remember in following motion to allow extra space ahead of the talent, what we called nose space before.

Pans are occasionally used to show a wide expanse of space. These pans are usually not as effective as simply going to a wider shot. There is a good example of a totally pointless pan on the CV4TT website. I'll admit I shot it. It's a pan across the

Seattle waterfront. Looking for a good place to end the pan, I also included a pointless zoom to a point of interest. And it's handheld, making a pointless shot even harder to view.

If you need to get from one point of interest to another, a cut would work better than a long pan.

Another common movement is a *tilt*. The camera pivots up or down. As with pans, the tilt should follow action. There is a useful tilt on the CV4TT website, in the Kisa video for this chapter. It follows the movement of the tree trimmer as he moves up to rescue the kitten. That shot also includes a slow zoom as the operator nears the kitten in the tree. I'll say a little more about that zoom a few paragraphs later.

Pans and tilts emphasize the importance of a good tripod head. A cheap head makes smooth movement very difficult.

Two movements involve actually moving the camera from one place to another. With amateur equipment, these are usually not feasible. A *dolly* move involves pushing the camera and tripod toward or away from the talent. Since our inexpensive tripods do not have wheels, we can't do that.

A *tracking* move involves moving the tripod to the left or right to follow action. On professional shoots, the camera mount actually rides on wheels and rails, with a person pulling or pushing the mount. You may see such equipment on professional shoots, but we can't afford that equipment, in general.

But you may need those movements. Using an office chair with wheels may provide a good substitute for a dolly or track. The floor has to be smooth and the pusher has to be very smooth. But it can work. The camera operator will probably hand hold the camera for this movement.

ZOOMS

It may be tempting to think of a zoom as a substitute for a dolly shot. And it may work. But be aware that a zoom and a dolly shot do not look alike. The zoom simply gets tighter, where the dolly shot actually changes perspective because the camera moves.

You will now want to view the Kisa video again. There is a slow zoom following the bucket as it moves up. You may also recall that I have recommended against zooms, in general, but here I used one. In this case, my judgment was that the zoom would not call attention to itself because it is following the movement that I want the viewer to follow.

If you are zooming in or out, note that you will need to tilt at the same time to maintain the rule of thirds composition. The zoom goes to or away from the center of

FIGURE 9.12. *The Initial Composition.*

FIGURE 9.13. *Same Camera Position as Figure 9.12, but Zoomed in Without Tilt.*

FIGURE 9.14. *The Result of a Zoom and Tilt Up.*

the shot. The images in Figures 9.12, 9.13, and 9.14 show the effect of a zoom into a shot without tilting.

These basics of camera work will help you compose your shots better and use camera movement purposefully.

■ ■ ■

In the next chapter we will see how we use light and lighting to create great video.

CHAPTER

10

LIGHTS AND LIGHTING

Video depends on light. It's our basic raw material. Light hits our subject and is reflected into the lens. The CCD changes the light into an electrical signal that, after some processing, is recorded as video. Using light well and controlling light are critical to making good video.

In this chapter, we'll look at characteristics of light, and then see how we can light our scenes to best effect.

COLOR AND INTENSITY

All light is not the same. We can describe light as soft, bright, or harsh or use terms like spotlight or floodlight. In describing lighting for video, we'll use a fairly specific vocabulary so we can describe and specify light in ways that we all understand the same way.

Light has intensity. Some lights are brighter than others. Sunlight is very intense, while the light in a fine restaurant may be quite dim. The camera needs some light, although modern cameras can get by with very little light. Even though the ads describe low light capability, the image will often improve with additional light. Our task is to add lights carefully, to preserve the appearance of the scene while improving the quality of the video image.

We can measure light using a light meter, but since our cameras most often do not have marked exposure controls, a light meter may not help much. What we will need to pay attention to is what the image looks like in the viewfinder and what we see with our eyes.

We will often control light intensity by selecting the light source for artificial light and by positioning the light to control its intensity at the subject. We'll come back to this topic when we talk about lighting setups.

Before we go on, we need to talk about color temperature. In video we can work with almost any color light, as long as it is consistent. Mixing colors will give us trouble. But first let's define and give examples of light color.

Color of light may be a new concept for you. The eye and brain compensate for a wide variation of light color and we don't necessarily see the difference in most situations. The camera does not adapt as easily as the human eye and brain do, so we have to be careful about our sources of light to avoid strange images that don't look at all like we expect them to.

If you have changed some of the lights in your home to energy-saving compact fluorescent lights (CFL), the color of the light may have become evident. Many people do not like CFLs because some are not very flattering. Some people do not like them in bathrooms and bedrooms, but will tolerate them in kitchens and hallways. It's because of the color.

Traditional incandescent light bulbs (the standard screw-in bulbs that get hot in use) have not changed much in over one hundred years. They produce light that is fairly yellow to orange in color. It's considered to be a warm light, one that we find flattering to people's appearance. Daylight, on the other hand, is more blue in appearance, especially in shade under a clear blue sky, as when the sun has gone behind a building, but the subject is still under a blue sky. Photographers call this condition "open shade," and it has very blue light.

Some light bulbs, and tubular lights used in specialty fixtures (see Figure 10.1), are called halogen lights, quartz lights or, more accurately, tungsten halogen lights. These are not as yellow as traditional bulbs and last longer. They produce good light for video, as it is bright, renders colors well, and can often be used in standard light fixtures, preserving the appearance of normal lighting.

We can describe the color of lights in a standard way, by referring to the color temperature in degrees Kelvin ($^{\circ}$K). This measurement refers to the temperature of a theoretical black body radiator as it gets hot enough to emit light. The table below shows some typical color temperatures.

Traditional incandescent (old)	2800 $^{\circ}$K
Traditional incandescent light (new)	3000 $^{\circ}$K
Halogen (quartz)	3200 $^{\circ}$K
Sunlight (noon)	5600 $^{\circ}$K

Note that traditional incandescent bulbs get yellower as they age. The tungsten boils off the hot filament and deposits on the glass envelope, darkening the bulb and changing its color.

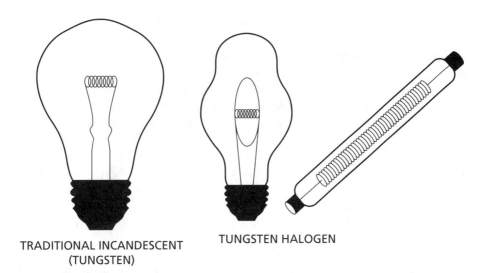

TRADITIONAL INCANDESCENT
(TUNGSTEN)

TUNGSTEN HALOGEN

FIGURE 10.1. *Incandescent, Halogen, Tubular Lamps.*

A virtue of halogen lamps is that the tungsten does not deposit on the quartz glass, remaining in the inert gas in the bulb until the bulb cools. Then it re-deposits on the filament, in a way that lengthens the life of the bulb and preserves its color. A problem with quartz halogen lamps is that the quartz glass capsule may shatter explosively. In some lamps, that capsule is enclosed within another glass outer shell as a safety measure. But with many lights, the quartz is open to the air. It is really important that you never touch those, even when installing them in the lighting device. Use a clean cloth or paper towel so the oil from your skin does not get on the quartz glass. The oil will heat up rapidly and may cause the light to explode. For the same reason, any fixture with a bare quartz halogen light in it will have some kind of safety glass covering. If this breaks, replace it. DO NOT use the fixture without it.

I've omitted fluorescent lamps because they don't really yield true color temperatures. While all of the lamps I've described so far produce light by heating something (a filament or gases on the surface of the sun), fluorescents produce light by bombarding chemical phosphorescent coatings on the inside of tubes with ultraviolet photons. (The photons come from passing electrons through a mixture of gasses.) The coatings emit light that depends on the specific chemicals in the coatings, each chemical emitting light in a few narrow bands of color. By combining different chemicals, the manufacturers try to produce pleasant light. Some will mark the packages with the equivalent color temperature (a rough estimate), or give them descriptive names, such as "warm white" or "daylight." The range of temperatures may range from about 3000 °K for warm white to about 6000 °K for daylight fluorescents.

The difficulty with fluorescent lights gets worse in typical buildings, where replacement lights are purchased on a lowest bid basis, with no regard for matching colors.

Thus, we see classrooms, labs, and offices with fluorescent lights of several different colors, depending on when they were purchased.

Mixtures of light sources, with different color temperatures, sharply degrade the quality of video. There are color samples of mixed light sources on the CV4TT website. The effect is strange, as different parts of the scene take on different colors in unexpected ways. The camera may attempt to correct it using auto white balance, but not well.

There are two key lessons from this discussion. One, avoid mixed lighting sources, such as daylight and incandescent in the same scene. Such a mixture might occur in an interior shot that includes a window, allowing daylight into the scene

The second lesson is to avoid fluorescents. Most often, if possible, we should just turn them off and supply our own light. The results will be better. When we can't turn them off, or we can't supply our own light (the area is too large, such as a factory floor or gym), white balance the camera for the fluorescent lights and don't introduce any other light into the scene.

A second characteristic of light is how sharp or diffuse it is. Reflected light, or light from a shaded lamp, is fairly diffuse, meaning it doesn't cast sharp shadows. Sharply focused light, as from a point source like a small halogen bulb or from a spotlight, casts sharp shadows. We need both kinds of light. In the next section we'll talk about lighting equipment and how to use the kinds of light they produce.

BASIC LIGHTING EQUIPMENT

For our purposes in this book, we do not need to consider the wide variety of expensive lights available to the professional video industry. We don't have the money or space for them. Instead, we'll look at on-camera lights, light kits, and what we can find at the hardware store.

First, let's define some terms. Floodlights produce diffuse light (soft shadows) over a wide angle. They flood the area with light. Spotlights produce sharp shadows and a fairly narrow beam of light. Because the light is spread out less than with a flood, they produce brighter (more intense) light over the area that's lit.

On-camera lights are convenient. They attach to the camera, usually using a shoe mount. Some may be powered by the shoe mount, but most require external batteries. The one shown in Figure 10.2 is small, inexpensive, and powered by the camera. Thus, it sharply reduces battery life.

The newest on-camera lights use arrays of LEDs (light emitting diodes) that are very power-efficient, meaning the battery will last longer than with halogen lights. They are also expensive, although we can expect prices to come down as manufacturing ramps up. They are available in several color temperatures, and some come with filters to change the color temperature.

While the on-camera lights are convenient, the disadvantage is they produce a very flat light, looking a lot like the light from an on-camera flash on a still camera. They

FIGURE 10.2. *On-Camera Light.*

produce no shadows or modeling, because they are right at the camera, so the light just bounces straight back.

Lighting kits are made to be portable and efficient. They normally include two or three lights and folding stands. These lights are usually floodlights, although some use reflectors to create a beam that's closer to a spot. Few have the lenses necessary for a true spot light. Almost all use quartz halogen lamps. An example is shown in Figure 10.3.

This lighting kit has a travel case, three lights, and stands. While the lights look like spots, they have no lenses. They produce a wide-angle light (flood) that is noticeably brighter in the center. With that characteristic, they can be used as spots for some purposes.

The stands are lightweight. Most teams use duck tape to tape them to the floor to avoid falling lights. The cords are short, making extension cords necessary. The cords need to be tied to the base of the stand so that a pulled cord is less likely to knock the stand over.

These lights also include two-way barn doors. These allow us to control where the light goes by adjusting the edge of the beam. In lighting a scene with a student in front of a computer, we wanted light on the student but not on the computer screen. The barn doors helped limit where the light went.

The lighting kit in Figure 10.4 has two lights, the rectangular one very definitely a flood and the other functioning more like a spot, although it has no lens. The spot uses a small quartz halogen bulb placed in front of a curved reflector that narrows the beam.

FIGURE 10.3. *Lighting Kit.*

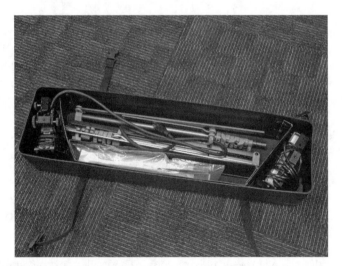

FIGURE 10.4. *Smaller Lighting Kit.*

Either of these kits works well for on-location lighting. They are very transportable, set up quickly, and are flexible in how they may be used. There are many choices in light kits. They work very well. For less money, you may be able to use lights from a hardware store.

FIGURE 10.5. *Work Light.*

A work light is a reasonably efficient flood light. These are inexpensive and very durable. Because they use quartz halogen lights, the color temperature will match other lights. One is shown in Figure 10.5.

Clip lights such as the one shown in Figure 10.6 can accommodate halogen lights. They are limited by the need to have something to clip them to. While shelves, doors,

FIGURE 10.6. *Clip Light.*

FIGURE 10.7. *PAR Light.*

and chairs provide good support, they may not be where we need them to be. Nonetheless, they can serve well and are very inexpensive. Because the reflectors are not carefully shaped to spread out the light evenly, using the clip lights may produce hot spots, that is, areas that are much brighter than the surrounding areas. Usually, we can deal with the hot spots by moving the light further away from the subject.

Other inexpensive lights include reflector spots and reflector floods. These are sometimes called PAR lights (Figure 10.7), for parabolic aluminized reflector. The spotlights often have small lenses molded into the front of the lamp, so they do work as spots, giving fairly well-defined shadows. The floods usually do not have the molded lenses. They can be screwed into clip lights or other portable lights and are available in a range of intensities.

Note these are available as traditional incandescent, halogen, and compact fluorescent. Make sure whatever you buy matches your other light sources.

BASIC LIGHTING SETUPS

Begin by turning off the room lights, especially if you're working in an office or classroom with fluorescent lights. We cannot see the effects of our lights with other lights on.

Most often we want the light we provide from our lighting equipment to look natural. Natural light comes from above the subject and viewer (think sunlight) and

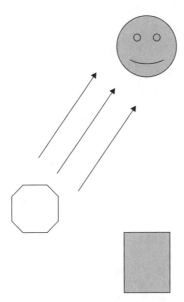

FIGURE 10.8. *Key Light.*

makes shadows that give shape to a person or object. Without shadows we get a flat image, with no modeling or features, which we saw earlier with the on-camera light or flash.

A single light, positioned higher than the subject and viewer (camera), somewhat off to the side of the axis between camera and subject, mimics the sun. We call this a key light (Figure 10.8).

It mimics the sun too much, because it causes very harsh shadows. We need to add some more light that will lighten the shadows. In sunlit outdoor scenes, this extra light is often supplied by light reflecting off the surroundings. Where there is no reflected light, we get deep shadows that may not even show any detail of the shadows on the subject because it is too dark compared to the sunlit area.

Here we add a fill light (Figure 10.9). If we have choices of lighting, the key light is a spot and the fill is a flood.

Since we may not have a choice of lights, we may diffuse the fill light using a diffuser, a sheet of fiberglass or other fireproof fabric that softens the light. We also want the fill light to be less intense than the key. We can achieve that by using a diffuser or moving it farther away from the subject.

Making the fill light half as bright as the key requires us to move it 1.4 times as far away. If the key light is 11 feet from the subject, moving the fill light so it is 16 feet away works nicely to cut the intensity in half.

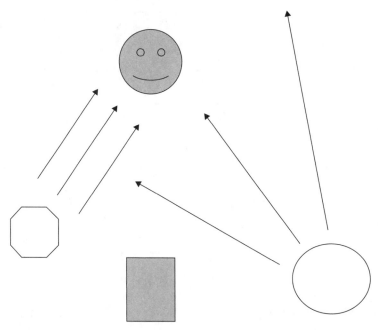

FIGURE 10.9. *Fill Light.*

NOTE

Some of you will have noticed that 1.4 x 11 is not 16. True enough. There is a sequence of numbers known to professional photographers and videographers. They use lenses that are actually calibrated with numbers for the aperture (how much light is allowed through the lens). That sequence is a decent approximation of the 1.4 rule (which is actually not 1.4 but the square root of 2, or 1.414...). The sequence is 1, 1.4, 2, 2.8, 4, 5.6, 8, 11, 16, 22, 32, 44, etc.). I use those approximations. If I have a light 8 feet from the subject and want to place an identical light so its light is half the intensity of the first, I will place it 11 feet away from the subject.

We can also reduce the intensity by bouncing the light off a white or neutral gray wall or ceiling. This trick is useful where we don't have the space to put the light 16 feet away. Many rooms in homes or offices are not large enough to place lights at such distances.

We may need a few more lights, although this basic key and fill setup will work for a lot of situations. We cannot judge the appearance of the lights without looking through the camera. Using a monitor, the LCD viewer, or even the viewfinder, if the camera has one, take a look at the talent and the lighting. Look at the face to be sure the shadows aren't too dark or the contrast between lit and shadow areas isn't too much for the camera to work with. Is the appearance pleasing? Do the lights (especially the key light) throw shadows on the background? Does the talent seem to blend into the background?

If there doesn't seem to be any separation between the talent and the background, we may need a backlight. This light is sometimes called a kicker or a hair light. But the idea is the same. Throw some light on the top of the talent's head from behind to make a halo or lightened area that separates the talent from the background. In color video, which we are doing most of the time, the backlight is less important than in black and white, but still may be helpful.

The backlight can be in line with the key light (Figure 10.10), which will keep it out of the shot. Or it can be in line with the camera, in which case it needs to be high to keep it out of the shot.

We may also want some general light to lighten up the background or the set. Without these, the talent may appear to be in a pool of light surrounded by darkness. Do not be tempted to just turn on the fluorescent lights in the room. These general lights need to be the same color as all the other lights.

We've talked about lighting with lights we place in the location. But sometimes the natural appearance we want may best be approximated by using the lights available in the room. This may be particularly true if we're shooting in a home, restaurant, or other more casual setting. The lighting should appear soft. The light also wouldn't normally be coming from above, as sunlight, but from lamps, sconces, or other lights in the normal setting. How can we use these?

They may produce enough light to shoot video, but likely they do not. Or it may be in the wrong places. We can start by replacing the light bulbs with brighter halogens. The light will be brighter but still appear to be coming from the expected light sources. Where these aren't enough, add some light from clip lights. We probably don't want to use the lighting kits, as they are too intense and will overwhelm the lights in the room.

LIGHTING PROBLEMS

Lighting doesn't always go easily. The basic three-light setup will work a lot of the time, but not everywhere and in every circumstance.

First, we'll address a common setup for an interview or dialog, where we have two people. The lighting we've talked about will light one person. That doesn't meet all of our needs. Often we need to light two people, as for a dialog or interview.

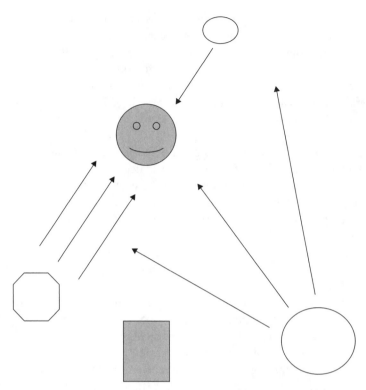

FIGURE 10.10. *Backlight in Line with Key Light.*

We probably don't have enough lights to provide key and fill for each of our talents on the set. If we're shooting with a single camera, as we most often are, we could light for one person and shoot the dialog with the camera on that person, say, the expert we've brought in for the interview, then set the lights again for the interviewer, and shoot the dialog a second time. Now we have plenty of video to edit together, including two takes of the dialog.

There is an easier way to do this, called cross-key lighting, shown in Figure 10.11.

We can place the camera at position C, which allows shots of the expert as well as over-the-shoulder shots that include the expert and the interviewer. Or the interviewer, if using a swivel chair, can rotate to face the camera. From that camera position, Light B serves as a key for the expert. Light A, which will later serve as key for the interviewer, is a fill light for the expert.

Here's how it works. Shoot the interview, with the camera in position C, so we can get medium shots and close-ups of the expert and wider shots that include the shoulder and head of the interviewer, over the shoulder. (The interviewer faces the expert throughout.)

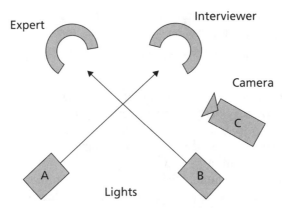

FIGURE 10.11.   *Interview or Dialog Set.*

If the expert has time and can stay for another shoot, or this is a dialog and both must be in the video all the way through, move the camera to the opposite side, facing the interviewer. Now Light A is a key light for the interviewer and Light B is a fill light. Shoot the interview again. Likely the expert will say things somewhat differently, or the interviewer might ask different questions. The editor will have a lot of good video to work with.

Most often, though, the expert will not stay for a second interview, especially if the expert is a busy person or who otherwise has a tight schedule. No matter. We have good video from the first take.

Use the second take, of the interviewer, to shoot him or her introducing the guest, asking questions, listening intently, nodding, looking perplexed, or other expressions as necessary for the interview to flow smoothly, and ending by thanking the guest and closing the segment. These continuity, question, and reaction shots can be edited into the first video. The reaction shots will be necessary to shorten the expert's talk, as we will see later in editing. It's called B-roll video and is essential.

Another common problem is mixed lighting, or very contrasty lighting. Mixed lighting will often occur when shooting in an office or home where there are windows. The outside sunlight is very bright, far brighter than even our lights from the lighting kit. And the sunlight is a different color, especially on a cloudless day. The expensive solution is to rent a very bright light, usually an HMI light, and diffuse it to provide general light over the whole set that is about the same color as sunlight. That's the solution used in the Michael and Lisa video.

Since that's not practical most of the time, here are some things to try:

- Shoot at night, so the outside light is not a problem.

- Close drapes or shades to block outside light. Note that blinds will not work as well, as light will come through the gaps between the slats.

■ Cover the windows with a neutral gray plastic sheeting to reduce the outside light, while still giving a natural appearance.

■ Reorient the shooting so the windows do not appear in the shot. Put them behind the camera.

Another daylight problem occurs when shooting outside on a bright day. The shadows cast by the sun are very dark, so the camera may not pick up much detail in the shadows. The camera will not handle great contrast as well as the human eye does.

In this case, get some white foam core board or other large, rigid white board from an art supply store. Make sure it's lightweight.

Have a member of the team hold the white board so it reflects sunlight back to the talent. In effect, use the white board as a fill, thinking of the sun as the key light. It works well, the color matches, and it's inexpensive.

■ ■ ■

With the knowledge in this chapter your team will be able to improve the lighting in videos without spending a lot of money. The improvement in the video will be noticeable, giving a professional look to your work.

CHAPTER

MICS AND SOUND

We've noted in a previous chapter that the built-in microphone or mic (say "mike") on the camcorder is not of much use and that you will need an external mic to get the best sound. It really makes a noticeable difference to use a proper mic, placed where it does the most good. It's the difference between being able to hear the talent or sounds that give the impression the talent is in a cave, behind a waterfall, or just very far away.

THE IMPORTANCE OF SOUND

While video is what we spend a lot of time talking about (even in the title of this book!), audio is an important supporting player. Sound can carry much of our content, whether the voice of a subject-matter expert, the music of a violinist, or the pinging of an out-of-tune engine in an auto repair video. Good sound can be important to the meaning of the video.

Sometimes sound is important to context. A silent video of a stamping plant will seem very strange to the employees of the plant. They know it's a tremendously noisy environment. The editor will want to fade the background noise down and out, but at least at the opening, the noise is part of the atmosphere of the plant. The chirping of crickets has meaning when played over a shot of a farmhouse at night. Contrast that shot with the one that includes an apartment building with audio of traffic sounds and an occasional siren.

We need sound. We need good sound, whether captured while recording or added later. To get good sound, we need microphones.

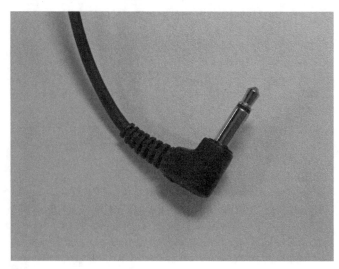

FIGURE 11.1. *Mini plug.*

KINDS OF MICS

There are hundreds of mics available. How do you select the ones you need? What about mics you may have already?

Let's narrow the field a little. As with everything else in this book, we're talking about consumer-grade mics. In this case it's not just because we're trying to save money, though we are. It's also that consumer grade camcorders have a mini-plug mic input and consumer grade mics have a mini-plug connector. They work together. Yes, it is possible to purchase an adapter that will allow professional mics with their 3-pin XLR connector (see Figure 11.1) to connect to a mini-plug input. There may be good reasons to use that on occasion. But mostly we want equipment that's compatible out of the box, without worrying about losing an adapter so that we cannot record on location when we want to.

> ## NOTE
>
> Why would we want the professional mics with their XLR connectors? If you need to run long mic cords or work in an electrically noisy environment like a hospital or factory, the professional cables (known as "balanced lines") and connectors are far more resistant to picking up noise than are the mini-plug mics (which are "unbalanced"). The noise will sound like clicks, static, or hum in the audio.

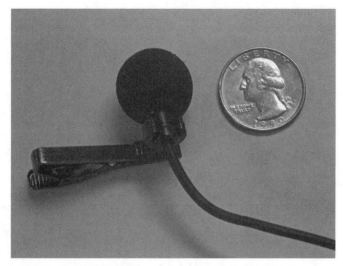

FIGURE 11.2. *Electret Mic, with Coin to Show Size.*

Within the category of consumer mics, we typically find two technologies, dynamic and electret (or condenser) mics. The tiny mic on your headset is an electret mic (Figure 11.2). They produce very high-quality sound, are very tiny, and are sensitive to even soft sounds. They can be a little fragile and require a source of electricity to work.

Dynamic mics are very durable and tolerate very loud sounds well. Rock bands use dynamic mics, as you might guess. They are larger than electret mics, so you often see these as the hand-held mics used by reporters or interviewers. They do not require a source of power to operate.

Electret mics need a source of power, as we've noted. Sometimes, especially in lower priced mics, that power comes from a battery installed in the mic or in a small pod on the cable. The mics don't need much power, so a small hearing aid–style battery will work well. Nonetheless, the battery will go dead if left on, so turn these mics off when not in use.

Some camcorders provide power (called phantom power) to the mic through the mic input jack. With those camcorders, there is no need for the battery. Some specialized camcorder mics are made for those camcorders and plug directly in or slide onto a special smart shoe adapter. I have a Canon shotgun mic (see Figure 11.3) that draws its power from a shoe on the top of the camcorder. It will only work with certain camcorders, those with the powered shoe.

Not all mics pick up sounds the same way. All mics pick up sounds from directly in front of them. Those that reject sounds from other directions are called unidirectional mics. That is, they pick up sounds from one direction.

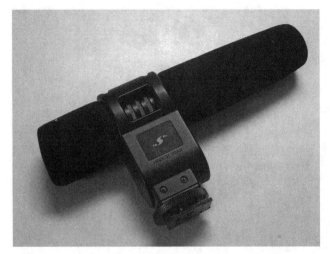

FIGURE 11.3. *Dedicated Shoe Mount Shotgun Mic.*

Some mics pick up sounds from all directions. These are called omni-directional mics. These are useful for recording a group of people, all about the same distance from the mic.

A few mics have other patterns, as seen in Figure 11.4. Some are cardioids; that is, they pick up sounds in a roughly heart-shape pattern. They reject sounds from behind the mic, favor sounds from in front, and will also pick up sounds from the sides.

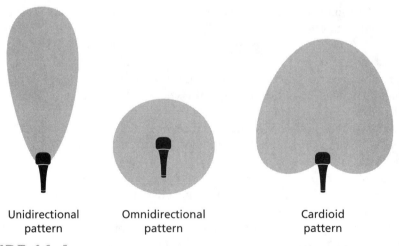

Unidirectional pattern   Omnidirectional pattern   Cardioid pattern

FIGURE 11.4. *Mic Pickup Patterns.*

Super-directional mics, or shotguns, pick up from a narrow angle in front and reject sounds from the side or rear. These mics are useful when you must use a camera-mounted mic and cannot get close to the talent. I have used shotgun mics when recording a visit to a school by a prominent person, when I had no opportunity to place a wireless mic (see the figures that follow) on the podium.

The importance of the pickup pattern is as much where the mic does not pick up sounds from as where it does. When it is not possible to get the mic close to the talent, we need to turn the volume up to hear the talent from a distance. Turning up the volume increases the level of everything the mic picks up, whether intended or not. Using a mic that picks up the talent, and little else, lets us turn up the volume without picking up noises we don't want, such as nearby conversations, rustling papers, or echo in the room.

When working outside, we'll want to use a windscreen on the mic. This is a cover that goes over the mic, usually made of foam or a furry material, that blocks wind noise and moisture from reaching the mic.

Indoors, a pop filter is useful, especially when the talent is close to the mic, as when recording voiceovers.

Beyond the specific technology of the mics, there are differences in shape and size that make a difference in sound quality also.

Shooting on location and gathering sound while we shoot, normally we want the mic near the talent and inconspicuous. Wireless mics fit the bill nicely. At $100 to $150, these cost a good deal more than wired mics, but are worth the extra. (Yes, you can find mics with 25-foot cords, but people trip over the cords and the crew constantly needs to keep track of them. Otherwise someone walks away with the cord attached, pulling over a camcorder when they hit the 25-foot limit.)

Wireless mics (see Figure 11.5) have two parts, a transmitter with an attached electret mic and a receiver with an antenna and a cord to attach to the mic input on the camcorder (Figure 11.6).

The talent clips the mic to a shirt or other handy bit of fabric or, taking a cue from stage actors, hides the mic in his or her hair or clothing. The wire connecting the mic to the transmitter also functions as the antenna, so keep it stretched out; don't bunch it up in a pocket. The transmitter may clip on a belt or waistband or go in a pocket, out of sight. Run the connecting wire through or under clothing to keep it inconspicuous, as shown in Figure 11.7.

Tape the receiver to the tripod or the camera strap; connect the cord to the mic input. Turn both devices on and you're ready to record.

Note that some wireless mics have a frequency or channel switch. If you find that the audio is noisy, try the other channel. The transmitter and receiver must be on the same channel. This switch is more commonly found in older wireless mics. In those, there may be an indicator light that shows green when the two are communicating; red when they are not.

FIGURE 11.5. *Wireless Mic Set. The transmitter is on the left, with the mic attached. The receiver is on the right.*

FIGURE 11.6. *The Receiver Attached to a Camcorder. Note the patch cord connecting the receiver to the mic jack.*

FIGURE 11.7. *Talent with Wireless Mic. The electret mic is clipped to his shirt. The transmitter is clipped to his pocket.*

The receiver usually has a jack for a headset or ear bud so the camera operator can monitor the sound. I do not recommend using it. Instead, connect your headset to the camcorder. Generally, it is better to monitor the sound closer to the point at which it is recorded so that, if there are any problems, they become apparent. For example, should the camera operator forget to plug the receiver into the camcorder, there would still be sound at the jack on the receiver. There just won't be any sound being recorded. A headset connected to the camcorder would be silent, so the problem would be evident.

I also recommend using an over-the-ear headset (Figure 11.8) for monitoring sound. These rather heavy headsets block outside sound, so the operator hears only the sound from the camera. Using lighter on-the-ear headset or earbuds allows sound coming through the air to be heard. It may be hard to tell the quality of the recorded sound, or even whether there is any recorded sound, when both sources are audible.

MIC SETUPS AND USE

Using a small, wireless mic on the talent is easy and reliable. There are other ways to use mics that may work better in some circumstances.

FIGURE 11.8.   *Over-the-Ear Headset.*

In a dramatic setting, having visible mics on the talent may be distracting, an unwelcome reminder that what we're watching is a planned, scripted video rather than something from life. The Michael and Lisa video on the CV4TT website is one such setting. The actors did not wear mics. Instead, a boom operator held a mic suspended from a pole above the table.

Professional booms are available, but a bamboo fishing pole will also work. Use an electrets mic for reduced weight and added sensitivity. Suspend the mic using fishing line from the end of the pole. Run the wire back down the pole. You could then use a transmitter or a longer cable to the camera. It is important to reduce the weight at the far end of the boom, since any weight at the end becomes very large to the boom operator due to the leverage of the long pole.

It is important that the boom operator be able to see a monitor showing the camera view. The operator needs to keep the mic just out of camera view—close enough to pick up the sound well, but out of the shot. It may also be possible to conceal mics in the set. Hide a mic behind or in a flowerpot, lamp, desk accessory, or a candy dish.

Conceal a mic in the actor's clothing, especially under a light scarf or shirt. Check the mic during walkthrough to make sure there is no sound from the mic rubbing against fabric.

VOICE-OVER VS. SYNC SOUND

It isn't always necessary to have a mic on the talent, or even in the shoot at all. Sometimes you'll add the narration later, in edit. When the script calls for voice-over, with an unseen narrator, we can record the sound later. We will still need a microphone, but the requirements are different.

When we record sound later, in post-production, appearance of the mic is not a concern. We want quality sound first. The mics may be larger, mounted on a mic stand or on a boom, and have a pop filter attached, which is a large disk between the talent and the mic.

What we need is a quiet location, really quiet. Just for a moment, sit and listen to the room you are in. (I'm assuming you're inside. If not, listen to the outdoor sounds.) While it may be quiet enough for reading, there are sounds around you. In my office, right now, I hear the fan from my computer and some noise from the ventilation system. Some people are talking outside my office.

A mic will pick up those sounds. We want to reduce those unwanted ambient noises. One way is to put the mic close to the person speaking, so the sound we want is much louder than the sound we do not want. We can also close doors, turn off the ventilation (for a brief time, anyway), or ask people to be quiet.

And we need a mic. We could use one of the mics we used for shooting video, and the budget may allow only one mic. So use it. But if your team has budget for one more mic, purchase a mic that's intended for desktop use. But before we consider which mic, let's talk technology again.

Microphones are analog devices. That is, the electrical signal available to the camcorder or other recording device at the mini plug varies in a wave pattern corresponding to the sound waves the mic picked up. Computers, such as the ones we edit video on or record sound on, are digital devices, recognizing only 0 and 1, not wave patterns. The analog signal from the mic needs to be converted to a digital signal. The camcorder has a digital to analog converter (A to D) to record the audio and video. When we view the video, a D to A converter makes it analog again so we can view and hear the video and audio.

Computers also have built-in A to D and D to A converters in the sound chips. On some computers, these are very good and make excellent recordings. On many, perhaps most computers, these converters are not very good. They are noisy (producing a lot of static or hiss) or inaccurate, producing sounds that are not a good representation of the original. The defects are often artifacts of the A to D conversion that leave the audio sounding brittle or harsh.

If you choose to use the mics you used for shooting, you will be using the A to D converter in the computer. Plug the mic into the mic input in the computer (usually pink) and record the voice-over. A free program like Audacity is a good recorder. The video editing software can usually record the voice-over and lay down the track for editing or tweaking later.

If, instead, the team is able to purchase a better mic for voice-overs (and can also use it for podcasts, webinars, and other times you need a mic for the computer), there are excellent mics available that include their own very good A to D converters. These connect to the USB jack on the computer because they present a digital signal and do not require further conversion.

Some of these mics use a slightly different technology, in that they are condenser mics. They are similar to the electret mic we discussed before, but are quite a bit larger. Common studio condenser mics are as large as a pop or beer can. They produce very high-quality recordings, although some are fairly delicate and can be damaged by rough handling. Many connect through a USB connector and have a built-in A to D converter that produces very good sound.

■ ■ ■

We have the basic equipment together, including a camera, lights, and mics. With some planning, we're ready to shoot some video. That's your assignment, which is described in the next chapter.

CHAPTER

12

YOUR ASSIGNMENT 2 EDIT IN CAMERA

Plan and shoot a simple video, probably no longer than three or four minutes.

Plan

Since we haven't talked about editing much, what you shoot will have to be your video. You will have no opportunity to fix things in edit. With this constraint, it is important that you plan your video carefully, because you will need to shoot it as it is to be viewed.

You will want to script this video carefully to make sure you can shoot everything in order.

Shoot

Start and stop the camera to allow cuts from one shot to the next. Do not use titles, fades, or any special effects that might be available on the camera.

Many students use this assignment to create a short instructional video. We have had several videos on how to bake a cake or make an appetizer. One student, whose husband was a skilled woodworker, made a short video on how to make tapered legs for a table. Others have shown how to do some basic checks on their car, such as oil level and tire pressure. A hiker showed how to prepare meals using just what he could carry in a backpack.

You cannot appear in the video, because you should be shooting it. So enlist your family and friends as talent. (If you're preparing food for the video, you'll need to share it with them.)

There are examples of student-produced edit in camera assignments on the CV4TT website.

SECTION

PRODUCTION

CHAPTER

13

SELECTING AND SURVEYING LOCATIONS

Few of us have the luxury of a studio for video. Most often we teachers and trainers make do with locations, that is, places that we use for video that are not created for that purpose. Offices, labs, homes, athletic fields, auditoriums, and other workaday spaces become our shooting locations. Selecting locations for our shoots can be time-consuming, and errors in location selection and surveying can delay our video production.

In this chapter we'll refer to scripts and then see what we have to find out and assure about our shooting locations. We'll also look at specific problems that can be encountered in some locations.

BACK TO THE SCRIPT

The left column of the script describes, somewhat generally, the locations we need. In the sample Grilled Flatbread script on the book's website, you will see the need for two locations. We need an exterior with a grill for cooking, and a kitchen interior for preparing the breads. Note that the viewer need not know the physical relationship between the two. In fact, the kitchen interior was shot in a commercial kitchen in a church that we were able to borrow for a day. Unlike many residential kitchens, the commercial kitchen is spacious, allowing room for cameras and lights.

The grill exterior is at my home, several miles away from the kitchen. Because we cut from one to the other at the beginning and end of the video, the viewer is likely to assume the kitchen and grill are near each other. That the two locations are some distance apart requires some planning, because we don't want to pack up and drive back and forth between the two locations.

The script will give some indication of the locations needed for the shoot. Most often, we don't treat the script as final until we know the locations, so the process is somewhat circular. Identify the locations from the script, survey and select locations, then modify the script to take advantage of the location and minimize any defects.

LOCATION SURVEY

Use the script to list the locations you need for the production. It might include interior and exterior shots. The interiors commonly include offices, labs, homes, or perhaps manufacturing facilities, retail locations, warehouses, and health care facilities. Often in making videos for training or academic instruction, the locations will be well known to the production team, as they are the places they work or locations related to the institution or enterprise. In other cases, the team will need to look for locations they are not so familiar with. A video for a research and development group may need manufacturing locations as a way of showing the relationship of product design to manufacturing constraints and resources. Or a video for a marketing class may have to be set in a retail location to tie marketing strategy to actual customer decisions.

Even in very familiar locations, when we're considering them for video production, we look at them with new eyes. We have to consider shots and camera locations, lighting, power, background noise, and access to the location.

SHOTS AND CAMERA ANGLES

Again, we need to look at the script. By now we've broken the script down so we have all the shots in this location gathered together.

Specifically, what are we shooting? What and where is the subject of interest, whether lab apparatus, machinery, people, or whatever the script calls for us to shoot? Knowing the location (or, possibly, how we want to rearrange the location to get the subject where it is easy to shoot) and the shots (close-ups, medium shots, whatever) tells us where the camcorder needs to be. Now we have to walk through the location, perhaps with a camcorder, to make sure we can get the shots the script calls for.

To make the shots work, it may be necessary to move furniture or change arrangements that look fine in the context of a room or office. In checking the shots, it is critical to see the camera's view. For example, two people sitting across a table from each other may seem very far apart in the video. We may want them to sit closer together, often closer than would be comfortable were it not a video shoot. Yet in the video, the characters will not seem strangely close together.

Many teams find it useful to take still pictures to remember the desired shots and how the furniture or equipment was moved to make it all work. Drawings, ideally drawn to scale, also are helpful when the team returns for the actual shoot.

LIGHTING AND ELECTRICAL POWER

With the shots worked out, consider the lighting. What light is available in the location? Many offices and commercial spaces have overhead fluorescent lights. These may be challenging to use for video. Review Chapter 10 on lighting, if needed.

If we can turn off the fluorescent lights, what's available? Windows offer very nice daylight, although usually from one side, leaving the other in relative darkness. Is there a place to put white foam core boards to reflect daylight back and lighten up the shadows?

Can we close draperies or blinds to get rid of daylight and use lights that we bring along? If so, is the ceiling high enough that the lighting looks natural? Or can we bounce light off the ceiling to create lighting that looks natural? To bounce light, the ceiling needs to be white or a neutral light gray.

Bringing our lights to the location raises questions about electricity. Lights draw a lot of power.

Identify where they can be plugged in. The portable lights I use draw 600 watts each. Two of those will just about take all the power available on a residential 15 amp lighting circuit (about 12 amps). Three will take almost everything available on a 20 amp office or residential circuit for outlets (about 18 amps). Since there is likely to be other equipment, computers, copiers, or other normal office or household lights plugged in, we usually want to spread the load out by running heavy extension cords to nearby rooms. By doing so, we try to spread the lighting load among several circuits and avoid overloading one.

The location survey must then include identifying power sources on different circuits.

In a commercial or office location, you will want to gain the permission and advice of a janitor, maintenance person, or building engineer about plugging lights in. This person will also be able to open the electrical panel in case you draw too much power and pop a circuit breaker, bringing a halt to your shoot and perhaps angering those around the shoot who are trying to work.

In a residential location, the homeowner may or may not know which outlets are on different circuits. The homeowner will almost always know where the breaker panel is to turn things back on, so trial and error may be the best approach.

SPECIFIC LOCATIONS: OFFICES

Shooting in offices can be surprisingly difficult. Most offices are small; 10 feet by 10 feet is pretty normal. Offices may contain furniture or office systems. The office systems, built-in work surfaces, storage, and shelves take less space but cannot be moved out of the way. Traditional furniture can be rearranged if we need space for camera, lights, or talent.

Working in such an environment, make sure the camera lens will go wide enough to get the shots you want with the camera in the close quarters of an office. An alternative may be to shoot through a doorway or an opening in partitions when there is office system furniture.

As you would do any time you're framing shots, look around the frame to see what is included in the shot. Clear away mementos, pictures, distracting bulletin boards, or other normal office contents that draw the viewer's eye away from the object of the shot.

If you're using lights, you will probably want to bounce the light from the ceiling since the lights will also need to be close. I have even placed the light behind the camera, which was in the doorway. We bounced the light off the white ceiling, providing reasonably good lighting in the small space of a faculty office.

You will need to coordinate your schedule with the office managers, who may want you to shoot in off hours to minimize disruption. Alternatives are to look for open office environments that may allow you to shoot and place lights over cubicle walls.

Make sure there is a break area, so that people not needed on the location have a place to go where they will not disturb others. Normally, we stock the break area with water, juice or soft drinks, as well as snack foods.

SPECIFIC LOCATIONS: HOMES

As with offices, a room that seems comfortable in normal use seems crowded when camera, lights, talent, and crew are added in, and suddenly that spacious living room or kitchen seems a bit too small.

Older homes may have limitations on electrical power, so you will want to check where you can plug in lights. In a home there may be alternatives, since many homes have visible light sources, such as table lamps or ceiling fixtures. You may be able to light the location simply by replacing the light bulbs in the normal fixtures with halogen lights. The effect will be that the lighting seems normal, but the video will benefit from the brighter, whiter light of the halogens. Do not let lamp shades or other fabrics around the light touch the halogens or become too hot.

Homes are more likely than offices to have distracting items on shelves and walls that you may want to move or avoid in shooting. Some artwork or knickknacks on shelves are to be expected and give personality to the room. Look at them through the eye of the viewer and make sure they're consistent with the content of the video and do not take the viewer away from the point of the shot.

SPECIFIC LOCATIONS: FACTORIES, SHOPS, WAREHOUSES, AND LABS

These locations present their own problems. Although there is often enough space to work and bright lighting, compared to offices and homes, we have other concerns in these locations. They include electrical power, noise, the atmosphere, and physical hazards.

Power is normally abundant in industrial or shop facilities. That doesn't mean all power is created equal. Because of the machinery in some locations, the power itself may be a source of electrical noise. Microphones, especially the inexpensive mics used with consumer equipment, are very susceptible to the electrical noise in industrial environments. It will sound like static, or perhaps a buzz, in the audio. You may decide that voice-over, recorded later in an electrically clean environment, would be the best way to go.

While some labs are whisper quiet, others, including shops, factories, and warehouses, are very noisy. A stamping plant, where metal is stamped into the needed shapes for appliances, automobiles, and other products, is among the noisiest environments to be found. Huge hydraulic presses slam heavy dies into sheets of steel to make pleasing and useful shapes out of flat metal. It's unavoidably noisy. Conversation is difficult and we would not want to record speech in that environment.

Even quieter industrial, warehouse, or shop space will have noise as a constant presence. Some noise would be appropriate in the video. To a person accustomed to a manufacturing setting, pristine silence would seem strange and artificial. So we will want to grab some wild sound for ambience. But we will want to survey the locations carefully to see whether recording dialog or speech is possible or what we may need to do with microphones to capture sounds in our chosen locations.

In some locations the air itself is worth paying attention to. In steel mills, some grain processing mills, farms, and other locations, dust is a constant presence. I've shot video in a glass bottle plant that had very small droplets of oil in the atmosphere. Occupational safety and health regulations mean that humans should be OK in any plant. If not, we can wear respirators. But our equipment may need some extra care, including placing it in plastic bags, with only the lens and cables coming out. We reach into the bag to operate controls. Minimizing reliance on mechanical devices, such as tape mechanisms, is also advisable in these settings. Use your camcorders with flash memory chips instead of tape.

While shops, labs, and other industrial spaces are generally safe, some present physical hazards that those who work there are aware of, but our video crew may not be. Those painted yellow marks on the floors show which areas are OK for walking and which are not. Robots, stamping presses, and other machinery may be surrounded by fences or electronic surveillance, which will shut the machinery down if intrusion by people is detected. Plant managers really dislike unscheduled shutdowns.

The crew needs to work with the people in charge of the location to make sure everyone is trained on the specific hazards of the location.

EXTERIORS

We often want to shoot indoors because we have more control than when shooting outside. With exterior shots we have to be concerned about the weather and constantly changing light. We try to leave schedules somewhat flexible, to allow for weather, unless you live and work in an area with good weather year-round. (That's one reason the early film industry left New York for Southern California.) In many parts of the country, seasons can affect schedules by months. If your video requires exterior scenes, showing summer and winter procedures, your timeline will be the better part of a year.

Bright sunlight, while it offers ample light, presents some lighting problems, simply because the light is so bright and the shadows so dark. We may use reflective panels, such as white foam core or poster board, to reflect sunlight back onto the talent from the side opposite the sun. This bounced sunlight will lighten shadows in ways we cannot achieve with inexpensive lights, which are far too dim to balance sunlight.

In the Grilled Flatbread video, we shot the exteriors at night, with a couple of lights, to simulate daylight. Figure 13.1 shows the lighting setup for this exterior. It works because the shot is in a confined location, with walls on two sides. If the grill were in

FIGURE 13.1. *Artificial Lights for an Exterior Scene, Shot at Night.*

an open area, the background would be dark and the effect of daylight lost. There is additional video on the CV4TT website explaining the location and the lighting.

That technique will not work unless the exterior is in a fairly confined space, since we do not have enough light to light up large areas. In those cases, unless you need sunlight, overcast days are excellent for shooting. There is plenty of light without the deep shadows from direct sunlight.

Daylight changes constantly, of course. As the day goes by, the apparent position of the sun in the sky changes from east to west, and the color of the light changes. Dawn and sunset present very different light from high noon.

COMMERCIAL AND RETAIL LOCATIONS

Most retail and commercial locations have restrictions on photography or video on the premises. They are concerned about competitors, use of trademarks, and other legitimate issues.

If you need to shoot in a retail or commercial location, get permission in advance. You may be required to shoot in off hours, and there can be costs involved for security personnel. If your video production is for the retailer or a supplier to the retailer, you should not have problems, although you are still likely to be required to schedule for off hours so you don't disrupt their business.

LOCATION RELEASES

Any agreements with the management of a location should be in writing. Commonly, the crew and management sign a Location Release, which specifies which locations can be used and when. Any restrictions should be included. The release explicitly allows the video team to shoot, reproduce, and publicly display images of the location in the video. The release may restrict what can be included in the shoot and where the video may be displayed.

Often the mere request for a signature will help identify who is really able to give permission to use the location.

You can find location releases on the web. As with any legal agreement, consultation with a lawyer is a good first step.

GREEN SCREEN—ANY LOCATION, ANY TIME

All this talk about locations is great, and we will often use real locations for our videos. But let's say our script calls for the characters to be in Piazza San Marco in Venice. Unfortunately our budget is inadequate to take crew and talent to Venice. But we can locate digital photos of the piazza that are in the public domain.

FIGURE 13.2. *Green Screen.*

We can shoot our talent in front of a green screen, shown in Figure 13.2. Then, in edit, we remove the green (actually make it transparent) and replace it with the photo, so the scene appears to be shot in Venice.

The technique works as well for less exotic locations that may simply be hazardous or difficult to get to, such as a mine, a planet, or any other location that you can find a photo of. Some editors will also let you use a video background for added realism.

We can buy green or blue cloth backdrops for video through many suppliers on the web. Make sure the talent is not wearing anything that closely matches the background color or that area will also go transparent. Actually, any color will work, but traditionally green and blue are used and the editing software is set up to use those colors.

■ ■ ■

With our locations identified and surveyed, we continue to move toward the actual shooting of the video.

CHAPTER

14

PLANNING THE SHOOT

The time spent actually shooting the video is the most expensive time in the project, even if you're not paying anyone. There are more people involved, more resources, and more equipment. It follows that the shoot must be carefully planned, with everything you will need in place when you need it.

PROPS

Props is short for "properties," the things that the talent will handle in the course of the production, such as a phone, recipe, or other item. Furniture or equipment that is used by the talent, such as the grill for the Grilled Flatbread Script on the website (see Exhibit 14.4 at the end of this chapter for the entire script), is a prop. Other items on the location, such as a potted plant that sits on the floor, that the talent never interacts with, is considered set decoration, not props. The distinction is that specific props must be available, while set decoration can vary.

The script is our guide to listing props. The script, broken down by location, lists what we need, although everything is not explicit in the script. Consider the sample Grilled Flatbread Script. First we'll look at the exterior scenes, which come at the beginning and at the end.

Reading the script, you will see we need flatbread, in this case, cooked flatbread just off the grill. Oh, yes, we need a grill. We will also need tongs. Start a list. See Exhibit 14.1.

EXHIBIT 14.1

Prop List for Scene 1

Scene 1: Exterior

    Grill

    Cooked flatbread, with grill marks

    Tongs

Because we generally want to shoot everything in one location at the same time, let's go to the last scene, which is the other exterior. The list in Exhibit 14.2 is a little longer, because the cook is baking the flatbread on the grill in this scene.

EXHIBIT 14.2

Prop List for Scene 3

Scene 3: Exterior

    Grill

    Uncooked flatbread

    Tongs

    Olive oil

    Brush

    Plate

    Bowl of hummus, or cooked chicken, or vegetables, finished sandwich???

At the end, the script casually refers to using the breads to make a roll-up sandwich or just dipping them in hummus. We could have some of those things available, or not,

ingredients, mixing bowl, wooden
spoon, prepared pizza dough

FIGURE 14.1.   *Note from Script.*

depending on the vision the producer/director has for the video. The script is not clear whether we should actually see the sandwich, ingredients, or the hummus. Check with the team to see how we want to finish the video.

When we move to consider the interior shots, the scriptwriter helpfully left a note (Figure 14.1) with some of the important props listed, but you immediately see that the note, helpful as it is, simply says "ingredients," so we'll have to read further to get the detail.

Reading further down, the voice-over lists the ingredients (Exhibit 14.3).

EXHIBIT 14.3

Close Up: table top—follow action

COOK: (VO)

You'll need flour, yeast, water, and a little olive oil. You may add some herbs to the dough, such as herbs de Provence.

Measure out one and a half cups of all-purpose or bread flour. Mix with a rounded teaspoon of instant or rapid rise yeast. That's about a half of a normal packet of yeast.

Add the herbs, if you're using them. And mix the dry ingredients.

COOK: (VO)

Add about one half cup of warm water and a half-tablespoon of olive oil and mix everything together.

Reading past the list of ingredients, we also note that we will need a measuring cup and measuring spoons. Read further to find additional props and complete your list.

The props for the flatbread video are all pretty common items and easy to locate. Some props present more difficulties. In corporate training videos, you may require prototype products that are hard to schedule, since there are often very few of them, or video requiring specialized equipment that is frequently in use in labs or production areas may present planning issues.

When you think you have everything listed, review the list and the script with other team members to make sure you haven't missed something or misunderstood what the script calls for. In many cases you will need a subject-matter expert to review the list and script. Someone not familiar with baking, for example, might miss props needed for the flatbread script.

PEOPLE

The Grilled Flatbread Script, with just one character, doesn't need much planning for people. The cook must be at each location throughout the shoot. The crew also needs to be present all the time. Most scripts aren't that simple.

The Michael and Lisa video is part of a larger production, with a cast of six people. The script breakdown includes three locations, the lunchroom where we see Michael and Lisa, an office area with cubicles, and a green screen studio. Each location was associated with specific dramatic vignettes, with different cast members. The office area included scenes with three co-workers. The green screen included only Anita, the learning agent, called, for purposes of this production, the virtual host.

Scheduling the talent paralleled the scheduling of locations. When we shot the lunchroom scene, we needed the crew plus the actors playing Michael and Lisa. When we shot the office scenes, we needed the actors playing the office co-workers. And, of course, we scheduled Anita for the studio shots.

It can become more complex, usually when dealing with large casts. We don't often deal with that problem with our videos. But there is one notable exception: dealing with officials, executives, or high-level administrators. We sometimes want them in our videos. A promotional video for our academic program required the dean to welcome participants and say some good words about the program. We were shooting a lot of video over the course of a day's shooting, but scheduled the dean for just fifteen minutes. That's all the time we could get. We set the lights using someone about the same size as the dean, so she could come in, review the questions and her notes, and sit in the chair we had set up. We started shooting. In a couple of minutes she was done and could go on to her next meeting.

EQUIPMENT

Just as we schedule people and props, we need to make sure we have the right equipment for the shoots. We'll typically need a camera, but different cameras have different features, so it's helpful to specify which one if you have a choice.

In addition, note which lights, if any, microphones, tripods, and extension cords are needed. Don't forget supplies, such as tapes, if your camera requires them, extra flash memory chips to allow for failures of chips, spare bulbs for lights, and duck tape to cover cords and affix light stands to the floor.

You will often want to have a computer with the script on it, to note any script changes that come up during the shoot. The editor will need that information.

SCHEDULES

All of this planning requires that the production team build schedules showing the locations, times, equipment, and people required for each shoot. The prop list, by location and scene, will also be necessary for planning.

You may want to break down the schedules by time of day. For example, the crew must be at the location before the cast, to set up lights, camera, mics, and other equipment. Then the cast can arrive, since we don't really need them earlier. While we do have lights set up, during walkthroughs and rehearsals, the lighting director can adjust lights so everything looks its best.

In building the schedules, consider the order that is best for shooting the scenes. It may not be the order in the script. For example, again we'll look at the Grilled Flatbread Script. The opening scene requires cooked flatbread, while the ending scene, also an exterior, starts with uncooked flatbread that we will cook during the scene. We can save time by shooting the closing scene first, then the opening scene. We'll cook the bread while we shoot the second exterior scene, then shoot the opening scene with the cooked bread. It doesn't really have to be hot and fresh as it comes off the grill for the shoot. It will look OK as long as we don't delay too much from one scene to the next, since the bread is most flexible when it is just cooked.

Then allow time in the schedule to take down equipment and pack it up. And if you're shooting a video about food, such as the Grilled Flatbread Video, allow time for everyone to sample the product.

■ ■ ■

Planning the shoot, in detail, allows best use of time when you are actually shooting and ensures that you haven't forgotten essential props, equipment, or people. It's worth taking the time to do it well. It's embarrassing, not to say a waste of time and resources, to be set up for a shoot, with talent and crew all ready, and you have to stop because an essential prop is missing. That kind of pain is avoidable, so be sure you're ready for the day of the shoot.

EXHIBIT 14.4

Complete Grilled Flatbread Script

VIDEO	AUDIO
MEDIUM: Exterior. Cook removes cooked flatbread from grill, using tongs, place on plate. Flatbread has distinct grill marks	COOK: Today were going to grill flatbread, one of humankind's oldest styles of bread, and one of the easiest to make.
MASTER: cook in kitchen, behind table CLOSE UP: pizza dough in bag	COOK: The dough is a simple yeast bread dough. You can make it easily or buy pizza crust dough from the grocery store.
MEDIUM: cook behind table	COOK: Because this is a simple dough, I'll show you how to make it from scratch.
CLOSE UP: cook	COOK: Some people get nervous about yeast doughs, but they are really very forgiving and are mostly about waiting while the yeast does its work.
MEDIUM: cook behind table	COOK: We'll just make a small batch, enough for four flatbreads.
CLOSE UP: table top—follow action	COOK (VO) You'll need flour, yeast, water, and a little olive oil. You may add some herbs to the dough, such as herbs de Provence. Measure out one and a half cups of all-purpose or bread flour. Mix with a rounded teaspoon of instant or rapid rise yeast. That's about a half of a normal packet of yeast. Add the herbs, if you're using them. And mix the dry ingredients. COOK (VO) Add about one half cup of warm water and a half-tablespoon of olive oil and mix everything together.

VIDEO	AUDIO
CUT-IN: Bowl	COOK (VO) The dough will start to pull together into a ball. If it's crumbly, add a little water. If it's sticky or too soft, add some flour.
MEDIUM: cook at table	COOK: That's what I mean about yeast dough being forgiving. If you're a little off with the ingredients, it's easy to correct things.
CLOSE UP: dough on floured table	COOK: Place the dough on a floured board or counter, and start to knead it.
CLOSE UP: kneading dough—dissolve to finished dough	COOK (VO) With the dough well covered in flour, press the ball with the heel of your hand, then fold it over on itself. Repeat until the dough is smooth and shiny. It should resist your pressure as it develops.
MEDIUM: cook at table	COOK: You could do everything up to this point with a bread machine or stand mixer, but for this small amount of dough, working by hand is almost easier.
CLOSE UP: dough in bowl	COOK (VO) Put the dough in a clean bowl, and pour a little olive oil over it. Turn the dough to coat it with oil,
MEDIUM: cook at table	COOK: and cover it. Place it in a warm, draft-free spot to rise, for about an hour. We want it to about double in size, but there is an easy way to tell when it's ready.
CLOSE UP: risen dough in bowl	COOK (VO) Press lightly in to the dough. If the dough doesn't spring back, it's risen enough.

VIDEO	AUDIO
MEDIUM: cook at table	COOK: Turn the dough out onto the floured board and punch it down. We want to break up the bubbles of gas the formed during the first rising.
CLOSEUP: cut the dough	COOK (VO) Cut the dough into four roughly equal pieces. Cover three of them. COOK (VO) Roll out the dough into an oval that's about one-quarter inch thick.
MEDIUM: cook at table	COOK: Thicker rounds will be chewier and flexible enough to roll up into a sandwich. Thin rounds will be crisp and cracker-like.
CLOSE UP: roll out dough	COOK (VO) The dough should be uniform thickness; otherwise it will be hard to cook evenly.
MEDIUM: cook at table	COOK: Roll out all four, and let them stand for a half hour or so. Cover them lightly; they'll rise a little during that time, making the flatbreads a little lighter in texture.
MEDIUM: Exterior, cook at grill	COOK: While the flatbreads are rising, fire up your grill.
CLOSE UP: set gas knobs to about 3/4	COOK (VO) Get it pretty hot because we want the breads to cook quickly, with nice grill marks.
MEDIUM: cook at grill, follow action	COOK: Brush the breads lightly with olive oil and place them on the grill, oil side down,
CLOSE UP: brush top side of bread	then brush the top side.

VIDEO	AUDIO
MEDIUM: cook at grill	COOK: Let them cook for a few minutes; you won't be able to flip them or check for doneness until they're close to being done.
CLOSE UP: bread getting bubbly—lift edge with tongs	COOK (VO) The bread should start to bubble and brown. You can lift the edge with tongs to check how done they are.
MEDIUM: cook at grill	COOK: When they have nice grill marks and have begin to firm up, flip them over to cook on the other side. They won't need quite as long on the second side.
CLOSE UP: takes bread off grill onto plate, using tongs	COOK (VO) Flip them onto a plate and they're ready to eat.
MEDIUM: cook at grill	COOK: These are best hot, but will be good at room temperature as well. You can fill them with chicken or vegetables for a great roll up sandwich, or just serve them with some hummus.

CHAPTER

15

THE DAY OF THE SHOOT

You have a final script, you've planned everything, the talent and crew are scheduled, and it's time to shoot. Let's first acknowledge that the title of this chapter makes an assumption that you can do your shoot in a day. That is probably a good assumption most of the time. But some videos are too complicated or have too many locations to do everything in a day.

We will continue using the Grilled Flatbread script and video as an example. This video can be shot in a day, but maybe you'll choose to take two days because it has two locations and it requires only a small cast.

The crew will need copies of the prop list, script, the site survey, and the schedules.

SET UP

We'll start with the kitchen interior, Scene 2.

The crew needs to arrive first, to set up the camera, mics, and lights. They will also move any furniture, distracting decorations, equipment, or other stuff noted in the site survey, so the location looks right and allows for camera, lights, crew, and talent to work effectively.

One of the first tasks is to set up a break area, including snacks, coffee, and soft drinks. The crew and talent will need this area when they are not needed at the shoot. It should be separated from the shooting location so noise does not travel, but not so far that it is inconvenient to move back and forth. In your small production, crew and talent might well be the same people. Still, a break area is helpful and makes it easy for people to feel appreciated and comfortable.

At each location there will be several setups. The script calls for some close-ups and some medium and wide shots. These require separate setups. The director will decide which setup to start with and the order of successive setups. Let's assume we want to start with a medium shot, which will shoot through the entire scene. That's a common practice, to get one continuous medium shot that the editor can use as a fallback if there is missing or unusable video, and it provides a complete take of the script.

As the crew prepares all the props for the scene, the director specifies where the props should be and where the talent is to stand. The director may mark the spot on the floor with tape, a step known as spiking. He or she may instead wait until the walkthrough with the talent to spike the spot.

The crew will set up the lights and the camera for the medium shot, noting exactly where the talent will stand at the work table. Since the talent needs to move somewhat to pick up ingredients or equipment, the camera operator will set up the shot to allow slight pans of the camera to follow the action.

They will refer to the site survey to make sure they plug the lights in to circuits that can supply the power without blowing circuit breakers. That mishap would bring everything to a halt while someone finds the building engineer.

As they set up, crew members will stand in for the cast to get the lights right. They will adjust them later, but now they need to put them in place. The lighting director will frequently refer to a monitor attached to the camera or to the camera LCD screen itself to see what the scene and stand-ins look like through the lens. The appearance as seen with the naked eye is an approximation of what the camera sees, and the only way to get it right is to view it as the camera sees it.

Setting up the mic (we only need one for this scene) is pretty simple. The easiest approach is to use a wireless mic. The sound person will want to make sure there are plenty of fresh batteries for the mic and receiver and to confirm the wireless mic works without a lot of static or interference in this location. We checked in the site survey, but things change in every location.

If for some reason you choose not to use the wireless, you can use a fixed mic placed in a hidden location on the table or a boom mic suspended above the talent, just out of view of the camera.

Get out all the media (tapes or flash memory cards) and write the title of the production, the date, and a number (1, 2, 3, etc.) on the label. Use them in numerical order. Write the number of the card or tape on the script when you start using it so you know where each scene and take is when the project goes into edit.

BLOCKING AND WALKTHROUGH

With everything set up, we can now do a walkthrough of the scene. The talent, in this case one, but in others you may have several, go through the scene, speaking all the lines or dialog. They are not in character, just reciting the lines, moving about the location as the script calls for it.

FIGURE 15.1. *Walkthrough for the Close-Ups. The lights have been moved and the camera repositioned to shoot close-ups of the bread preparation on the tabletop. The director, at right, is talking the talent through the shots.*

The camera operator and lighting director follow the action, stopping it as necessary to make corrections, offer suggestions, correct, or set spikes (tape marks) on the floor, so talent knows exactly where to be at each point. Where there are several characters in the script, we also watch how the characters interact and that the shot is available to show whichever character is important all the time. This positioning is known on the stage as "blocking," which simply means getting people in the right place so they can be seen when they are supposed to be.

This walkthrough is also a last-minute check to make sure all the props are where they need to be. Characters should pick up and use props as the script calls for them. In a video with consumable props, such as the ingredients in this script, do not pour out or mix ingredients. Just mimic the motion with the props. See Figure 15.1 for a sample walkthrough shot.

This walkthrough is not in real time, that is, it will take longer than the shot is supposed to run, because of the starting and stopping while lights, props, and camera are adjusted.

CAMERA REHEARSAL

With everything all set, we need to rehearse the scene. This is a final rehearsal. The talent is in character, speaking lines as the character speaks them. Most crews have the camera rolling for the rehearsal, since we can sometimes record shots in the rehearsal that don't recur later when we're shooting the "real" takes. The rehearsal is for the benefit of the camera operator and director as well as the talent. That is, everyone is rehearsing. The camera operator is following the action. The director is tracking the dialog and action, as well as watching the monitor. Someone on the crew is watching the script and listening, to note any deviations from the script.

With all that going on, the camera might as well be rolling. Before starting the camera, remember to set the white balance for the lighting. How cameras do this will vary, so look over the menus to find the setting for manual white balance. Then hold a piece of white paper in front of the lens, lit the same way the scene is lit, and adjust the zoom so the paper fills the frame. Then press the button to set the manual white balance. This step sets the camera for the lighting on the scene, rather than depending on the sometimes unpredictable automatic white balance.

If (when) the talent says something different from the script, normally we'll correct the talent so the take is faithful to the script. But sometimes the script just is hard to say or doesn't seem natural, so the director and subject-matter expert may decide to change the script. Such changes make the final version of the script, as produced. The editor needs the as-produced script to assemble the final video.

To help the crew and talent stay focused on the particular shots we're shooting, the rehearsal covers just those shots, not the whole scene every time. If the first take is a medium shot of the whole scene, rehearse the whole scene. If we're then moving to the close-ups, rehearse each close-up shot just before the real takes. Since you're running the camera for the rehearsals, the effect is that you're doing a preliminary take, and that's OK. Sometimes thinking of it as a rehearsal rather than a real take leaves the talent more relaxed, resulting in a better shot.

THE ACTUAL SHOOT

Then we shoot the video. It's almost anti-climactic by now. And with all the preparation, it should be. You'll shoot, log the time codes (if your camera produces them) or the date and time, and go on to the next shot. Between shots you may have to rearrange camera and lights. For extensive changes, send the talent to the break area, as you don't want extra people in the way.

If your shoot takes more than one day, you will want to secure the location between shoots. If it is a location that you're using in off hours that needs to be restored to its normal use between shoots, clean up after each day's shoot so the space can be used for its normal purpose.

AMBIENT SOUND

Great work! It may have been a long day, but we have our video. There is one more brief task that will make life easier for the editor. Record several minutes of the ambient sound in the location. Just ask everyone to be quiet while you let the camera run.

Every space has a distinctive sound, from the ventilation system, outside noise such as traffic, or equipment in the room. The refrigerators in our kitchen make noise that is almost always there. We need that ambient sound so that, during edit, we use the sound that we recorded. Maybe someone on the crew drops something and makes some noise. The video was great and we want to keep it. So we cut out the sound and overlay it with the ambient sound. Maybe we record voice-over at that point, over the ambient sound, so it sounds natural. If we just cut the unwanted sound out, the video is too quiet, quieter than anywhere else in the video. So we want that ambient sound to cover any such deletions.

TEAR DOWN

When you have all the shots in the can, that is, on tape or flash memory chip, put all the equipment away. Restore the location to a condition better than what you found. If you removed things from the location for the purposes of the shoot, put them back now.

- Clean up after yourself. Remove tape marks from the floor. If you moved it, put it back.

- Remove the tape or memory cards from the camera, place them in their case or other packaging, and put them in a safe place.

- Pack up camera, lights, mics, extension cords, making sure you take everything out you brought in. Clean up the break area.

- If the location needs to be secured, find the building engineer, manager, or other person who can close up after you leave.

Make it easy for the people or organization that loaned you the location to be able to help you again. If you are not good guests, you won't be able to use the location the next time you need it.

The good news is you've captured the video you need. We've completed the production phase and now move to post-production. It's been a lot of work and you now anticipate reviewing the takes in the edit suite to see what you have and how best to turn it into a video people will learn from and enjoy seeing.

CHAPTER

16

YOUR ASSIGNMENT 3 PLAN AND SHOOT

This is the first of two parts that will result in a completed instructional video. In this assignment you will plan and shoot the video. In the second part, in what is called post-production, you will edit the video and make a DVD.

This is a team project. In this video, as a team project, members of the team will take on different roles and may be the talent.

Plan

Create a treatment, script, shot list, and prop list for your video. Visit locations, even if they are very familiar to you, but look at them through new eyes. Look at them as locations for video. See what you will need to move, bring with you, or change to make the location work.

Shoot

Work through the script, in the order specified on your shot list. Set up, walk through, rehearse, and shoot. Record ambient sound. Write down any changes made to the script while shooting.

SECTION

IV

POST-PRODUCTION

CHAPTER

VIDEO EDITING

Editing is the process of turning the raw footage you shot into a video that someone will want to watch and learn from. It draws on your understanding of the content and of the instruction, plus a large measure of creativity to make the video interesting and effective.

One of our purposes in editing is to help the learner know what to pay attention to. We'll show the big picture for context and details for clarity.

ESSENTIAL SOFTWARE

Most computers include very basic editing software. On Macs, there is iMovie. On Windows, there is Movie Maker. These simple programs are not suited for serious editing. They are missing important features that are present in programs that cost only slightly more than free.

Sony, Pinnacle/Avid, Adobe, and Apple all offer feature-rich programs for $100 or less. This market is very competitive and the feature list grows every year for all of these products. At any given time, one or another will be rated top by several reviewers. I don't suggest buying a new product when the reviews now rank yours as third that year. The learning curve for any editor is important. Each has its own way of doing things, although some operations are similar. Since editing is so time-consuming, efficiency is important, and efficiency comes from being very familiar with the way your chosen editor works.

Figure 17.1 shows the interface from Pinnacle Studio, a fairly typical editor. The lower half of the screen shows the selected video, with the length of the clip indicated by the space it takes up on the timeline. The figure shows the timeline view. It can

FIGURE 17.1. *Pinnacle Studio.*

change to show thumbnails, usually used when initially selecting shots, using storyboard view, which is called "scene view" in Adobe Premiere, another common editor. The upper right area is the player, showing the current scene, player controls, and time. The area on the upper left currently shows the available video clips. That area changes depending on what the editor is trying to do. For example, if the editor is trimming a shot, the upper left area shows the shot, in and out markers, and times. When adding a title, the area changes to show the title, fonts, and other text editing tools.

Note that the editing software has broken the video into scenes. The upper left corner shows all the shots that were recorded, but has separated them into shots so the human editor can assemble them as desired.

The additional tracks on the timeline allow for adding titles, recording voice-over, and adding music.

Adobe Premiere Elements, a popular low-price editor, has a similar interface, shown in Figure 17.2. It shows the same features in a slightly different arrangement.

A list of minimum required features would include:

- Ability to import video from the cameras you use. Most editors import from tape and from files on flash memory cards. If you shoot video on a still camera, phone, or mini-camera like a Flip, make sure the editor can import the video you shoot.

- Edit in the formats you want to use. If you want full HD, like 1080p, and your camera shoots full HD, the editor will have to work in that format as well.

FIGURE 17.2. *Adobe Premiere Elements in Scene View.*

- Scene detection. The video files from the camera are huge. The editor must break the file into scenes so the editing can be organized. The editor does not want to break down an hour of video into the several hundred scenes it contains just to start editing. Some editors detect scenes as the file is imported; some do it as part of an analysis step that also checks the video for defects.

- Drag-and-drop editing is common, although how the software does it varies. Some will let you drop the scene anywhere on the timeline. Others will only let you drop in sequence, although it is easy to drop a scene between two scenes already on the timeline.

- Ability to lock tracks independently. There are times when we want to maintain the audio and replace the video, as when doing an insert edit. To do so, we must be able to lock the audio while editing the video track. Conversely, we will at other times need to lock the video while cutting or replacing the audio track.

- Correct minor problems in video and audio, such as under- or over-exposure, volume too low, some extraneous noises, and minor color correction.

- Record voice-over narration.

- Add sound effects or music.

- Produce output video for the devices, sites, or ultimate use that is intended, whether YouTube, Flash, or HTML5 video, portable devices, DVDs, and a long list of others. Note that, for some of these outputs, the editor may render an AVI or other generic file, which then requires further processing such as the Adobe Flash Video encoder.

Note that video editing is very demanding of your computer. Buy the largest disk, memory, monitors (yes, two monitors—one to display the editor and one for the script), and processor you can afford. Computers designed for gamers are usually good for editing because they have very good video cards and lots of memory (RAM).

With the editing software and computer selected, let's look at some editing tasks.

A SIMPLE EVENT SHOOT

At its simplest, let's consider the event video. You attended commencement and shot video of the ceremonies. Because this is an event shoot, the sequence of video is set by the event. You shot it as it happened, so your shots are in the sequence they occurred and largely in the sequence you will want to show them.

I say "largely" because you captured some video that could be used anywhere, your B-roll, that you'll need to cover cuts and lend visual variety in longer sequences. The graduation speaker was good, as speakers go, but you don't want to impose on your audience by playing the whole speech. You want the highlights. The parade of graduates marching in to "Pomp and Circumstance" gets pretty repetitive after the first dozen or so. It's your skill as an editor that takes the hours-long ceremony and distills it down to the thirty minutes you want to show to a general audience.

Because you shot with a single camera, you don't have the whole ceremony anyway. Some of the time you were moving to a better vantage point for the next part of the ceremony. You shot the marching faculty and graduates from the front, at the aisle, to better capture their serious, but delighted faces. Then you moved to the front row of the balcony to capture the band performance and the speakers. And back to the main floor on the aisle to get shots of the graduates marching out. The positions are shown in Figure 17.3.

Our editing goal with this scenario is to put together a video that tells the story of the graduation in a coherent, attractive video. We'll assume you shot this with an eye to later edits. So your shots of the graduates and dignitaries marching in had a variety of perspectives, achieved with changing the zoom setting on your camcorder and changing your position. So you can trim these scenes to show some of the top officials (politically, you probably want the president or principal) then a selection of faculty and graduates.

Open the video file in the editor. If you used tape, you'll capture the video from the tape to your hard drive. If you used SD card or hard drive, copy the video file to your editing computer. Most editors can be set to cut the video into scenes, so you'll have thumbnails of each scene.

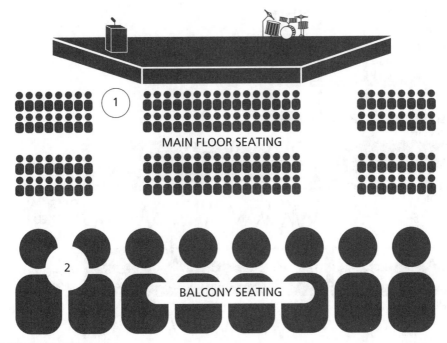

FIGURE 17.3. *Auditorium Shooting Positions. Position 1 is at the head of the main floor aisle. Position 2 is toward the front of the balcony, for a view of the stage.*

Review your video and make notes as to which shots you do not want to use because of some serious quality issue, and which scenes are really important because of what they contain.

Begin with the graduates' march in. First, drag a long (long in time, not focal length) shot to the timeline. We want this scene there to get a continuous musical track of "Pomp and Circumstance." If we don't have this sound track down, every time we cut to get the right visual, we cut the music and the result is jumbled sound. Every cut results in a transition to a new section of this very familiar piece of music.

With the music in place, lock the audio track so your changes to the video won't disrupt it. Select the other march shots you want to include. You might want to begin with a wide shot that shows the auditorium, called an establisher shot. It shows the context of the video. Then go to a mix of medium shots and close-ups.

Cut out sections of the original video and replace them with the shots you want to include. Your editor has something like a razor that lets you split scenes on the timeline so you can delete original video and insert other video in its place (Figure 17.4). To relieve the monotony of marching graduates and faculty, insert some shots of the

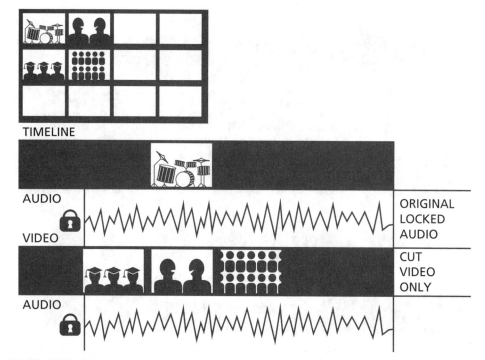

FIGURE 17.4. *Insert Edit. The original timeline has one long shot, in which we recorded the music. The second timeline, after the edits, keeps the original audio, but cuts in audience shots.*

audience or dignitaries on the stage. Keep the pace of cuts here fairly fast, to capture the energy and excitement of the graduates.

Your result will have a continuous run of the music under a variety of shots of the marching graduates, dignitaries, and faculty, with cut-aways to show the audience and stage.

This sequence, beginning with an establisher or wide shot, followed by closer shots, telling the story with mixed shots, then backing out to wide shots at the end of the sequence, is called "analytical" editing. It's a good place to start when you're trying to work out a sequence of shots for your video.

Continue working your way through the graduation ceremony. Edit for content first. That is, select the shots that tell the story of the ceremony: introductions of dignitaries, speeches, the conferring of degrees, and musical selections. We do not want to include everything, but we do want to tell the story in an engaging way.

The resulting video, with the highlights, is called a rough cut. It's not finished, but includes the content you've decided to show.

Now we want to improve the video. Some scenes run too long. The music was good, but we only want to show a few minutes of it. The speaker was interesting as graduation speakers go, but, again, we want to trim it down. We can't watch all of the 232 (or however many there are) graduates cross the stage and receive their diplomas.

Here's where the editor turns too-long and too-much into interesting and enjoyable. Some scenes do not have specific sound associated with them (students marching in or out) and some do, such as musical selections and speeches. That is, the music and speeches need to maintain synchronization. The words and mouth movements must match, as the music and instrumentalists' and conductor's actions must match. Frame by frame.

Shots that require synchronization require more careful editing than those that do not. Let's first deal with those that do not.

There are numerous shots here that include applause. We want to trim these. Even though there is a specific sound, it's not synchronized. It is "wild sound," that is, general sound that does not have a specific visual reference, other than general shots of an audience clapping. So we shorten the shots (Figure 17.5) that include applause to the length we want, at most a couple of seconds. If we just trim the scene, the applause will cut off abruptly and sound unnatural. After we trim the shot, we will adjust the

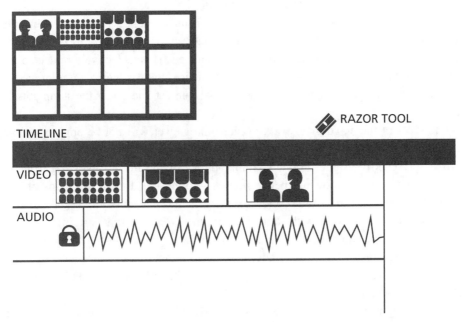

FIGURE 17.5. *Use the Tool to Cut a Shot, Allowing Other Video to Be Inserted.*

volume (level) of the sound by editing the sound track itself. Depending on your editor, the technique varies, but what we want to do is fade out the applause. It may be done with a sound mixer or on the timeline itself, but the result is the same, a pleasing fade out of the applause as the next scene begins.

Another scene that might be synchronized or might not is the graduates marching across the stage to receive their diplomas. While there is probably someone announcing names as the graduates walk up, we might decide not to use that audio, since the point of this scene is to show typical graduates walking across without giving undue prominence to any specific ones.

We can remove the audio with the announced names and paste in music from other places in the video to result in a good scene that effectively tells the story.

Most scenes, however, require synchronization. The speakers and the music have specific visual referents, whether the person speaking or the musicians. Let's deal with the speakers first.

We'll need to shorten the speeches, while still including the essence of the content. First we edit for content and flow. We do that by listening carefully to the speech, identifying the key ideas and memorable phrases, and cutting everything else out. This sort of editing requires a clear understanding of the speech, even to the point of outlining it to make sure we're clear on the major points and key ideas.

Once we've cut it down, we have a speech that makes sense in the audio, but the video is full of jump cuts and is not especially coherent. Yet we can't lose synch with what we have. Lock the audio track so it doesn't change. Then selectively replace parts of shots from the video with cut-aways to the audience, the graduates, the dignitaries, or even wide shots of the stage, to maintain visual interest and cover the jump cuts in the edit.

Wide shots of the stage may work, because the viewer will not be able to see the speaker's face well enough to judge whether it's in synch.

Music presents the same problem. Some actions of the musicians and conductor must be in synch. Violin bowing, percussionists striking the drums, close-ups of any instrumentalist, and gestures of the conductor must be in synch. If you're not a musician and can't see the synch, work with someone who does. Because this is a single camera production, avoid shooting close-ups unless you know you can edit the shots in a way that makes sense musically. Some higher-cost video editors can bring music or voice into synch if the video and audio aren't too far off. But it's better to keep things in synch from the beginning.

If your thought now is that editing is time-consuming, you're right. Doing it well, creating an interesting, visually appealing video that tells the story and conveys the excitement of the ceremony takes time. The result will please the audience.

A PLANNED INSTRUCTIONAL VIDEO

More common is a planned video, in which you've created a script and storyboard, then shot the video using a shooting script and shot list. To help in edit, you've marked up the script with any changes and included time codes or slates so you know what assets you have when you begin editing.

Again, open the video in the editor, review your video assets, and make notes about which segments you don't want and which to include.

If your script has voice-over narration, that is, an unseen narrator, except for perhaps opening and closing scenes, you'll make a rough cut to show a consistent, sequential visual story, then fine-tune with a final edit.

Begin with your A-roll shots. Remember, these are the ones that carry the visual story of your video. With a lot of medium shots, piece together your narrative, in the sequence you want it to be viewed, by dragging video to the timeline. At this point, don't worry too much about pace or even small errors in the content of the video or audio.

After you have a good edit, then you can record the voice-over. The editor software probably has a facility to add narration. In a quiet room, with a quality microphone, record the narration. Or record to a separate application and lay down the audio track and import the audio to the video editor. While you're recording, also record some silence. That's the ambient sound in the room. Record thirty seconds or so. You'll need this in editing the sound if you have to add a few seconds here or there between sentences or paragraphs to have the narration match the video action. If you just insert blank audio (no sound at all), the absolute silence will be noticeably quieter than the ambient sound and draw attention to itself. The ambient sound will make the edit sound as if the narrator simply paused.

With the narration track laid down, then go back to editing to adjust the video and narration to each other.

With the narration in place, it will be easier to insert cut-ins and cut-aways, as the insert points will be clearer. While the narrator is describing a detail, insert a cut-in to show exactly what the narrator means. While the narrator is talking about something more general, go to a cut-away or a medium shot. We'll discuss cut-ins and cut-aways a little bit later in this chapter.

If your script calls for narration by talent on camera (TOC), then you'll need to edit the rough cut you just produced to achieve a consistent, sequential narrative from the talent. That is, you're editing to get the audio right first. You may even have shot the whole script once through with a sequence of medium shots, primarily to capture the audio narration.

Once you have the rough cut, you'll improve the video.

First, because we didn't worry too much about pace in assembling the rough cut, you'll now remove video that is not correct, or is too slow, or doesn't advance the story along smartly. If your script calls for narration, whether voice-over or talent on camera, overall length and scene length will be largely determined by your script. Make sure the scenes as edited match the length of the required narration for each scene.

If you have talent on camera (TOC), the overall length is right because you edited for the sound. But some scenes may not be visually paced well, or be boring, or not show detail. Here's where we need the B-roll.

CUT-INS AND CUT-AWAYS

For both of our videos, TOC and voice-over, our task is now to improve the rough cut. Both consist of mostly medium shots. We will need some close-ups to show details and add interest. These close-ups are cut-ins because they cut into the scene. In some places we want to cut away, to show something that's happening outside of the scene, perhaps a reaction shot of someone listening, or to show something that is happening at the same time with other characters, as might be useful in a dramatic video

The basic technique for cut-ins and cut-aways is the same, as far as the actual edit. Both are accomplished with an insert edit. Because our audio is right in the rough cut, we'll lock the audio track so when we cut into the video, we don't disturb the audio. With the audio locked, delete a portion of the video and drop in some video from the B-roll.

When we shot the voice-over video, a demonstration of a procedure, we also shot close-ups of the procedure. We insert these into the video at appropriate points to show detail. In the dramatic video, we can cut away to show simultaneous events that relate to the main narrative, such as a crowd shot.

INTERCUTTING

Sometimes it is necessary to show simultaneous actions occurring in two or more places. You're shooting a demonstration to show how to measure blood pressure with a cuff. Once the cuff is in place, you'll need to show the talent squeezing the bulb to blow up the cuff. You'll show the cuff itself as it inflates. The actual pressure is shown on a gauge. You'll cut back and forth from the cuff to the gauge to the bulb, with occasional cuts to the talent's head to show listening at the stethoscope. Since all of these things happen simultaneously, intercutting keeps the viewer's attention on all of them. Recording the sound helps the viewer learn what to pay attention to in order to know when the cuff is inflated sufficiently, how to slowly release the pressure, and what to listen for and observe to measure systolic and diastolic pressures.

From an instructional perspective, there are several things the learner needs to attend to, and your editing helps direct attention to those. The sound heard in the stethoscope will be recorded and added in because it is so important. The video editing will be paced to the sound, so that as the cuff reaches the needed inflation, the learner hears that the blood is no longer flowing. It is important at that point that the video show releasing the valve so the pressure can begin to come down and then cut to the gauge to note the pressure at which blood begins to flow again.

GREEN SCREEN

Video editing software allows you to place your characters in front of any scene you want, using a technique known as green screen. Actually, the screen can be blue as well, but we call it green screen.

In the shoot, we place the character in front of a green backdrop, as in Figure 17.6. The backdrop can be purchased from video suppliers. In edit, we make the green transparent, so an image placed behind the character looks like a background or location, as shown in Figure 17.7. There is a fuller description of the green screen shoot in Chapter 13.

In the editor, the background video or still image goes in one track and the green screen scene in another. Select the green screen option, which may be called chromakey in some editors, and select the green or blue background color as the color to become transparent.

In edit, there are some choices to be made to make the green screen effect work as intended. Because of shadows or uneven lighting, the green backdrop may not appear to be a consistent color. The editing software allows some range of colors to go transparent.

FIGURE 17.6. *Talent in Front of a Green Screen, with a Floodlight.*

FIGURE 17.7. *The Edited Result of Green Screen. The talent was shot in green screen. The background images were added in edit.*

Courtesy DaimlerChrysler Financial, Production Café, The Emdicium Group, Inc.

Too narrow a range and some parts will not go transparent. Too broad a range and some colors on the character may go transparent, creating an odd effect.

Other choices allow for a degree of smoothing to avoid jagged edges between the character and the new background scene and degree of transparency of the background.

■ ■ ■

The mechanics of editing are fairly simple. Most often you drag and drop your shots onto a timeline, then trim the shots to improve pace, and highlight what your learner should pay attention to. Cut-ins and cut-aways further help direct attention. Intercutting helps clarify simultaneous actions. The artistic and creative aspects of editing demand time and patience to produce an esthetically pleasing video that is effective as instruction.

CHAPTER

18

AUDIO EDITING

Because video is such a visual medium, it can be easy to neglect the audio. But especially when we're dealing with instructional video, sound can be really important and worth the effort it takes to do well.

In this chapter we'll expand on the editing process to include specific issues about editing sound. In the last chapter, we showed how the editor will often edit the video clips to obtain a coherent audio narration, whether recorded by the camera in the shoot or added later as a voice-over track. So we won't go over that content again here.

In Chapter 17, we described two ways of editing, one in which we first edited for continuity of the sound track, then edited the video, and a second in which we edited the video, then recorded the narration. Keep those processes in mind as we work through this chapter, which is concerned with improving the overall sound.

CLEANING UP CAMCORDER SOUND

The basic audio source is the sound recorded by the camcorder in the video shoot. But rarely is camera audio all your project will need. The audio captured in the video shoot may contain voices from talent on camera, music, background sounds, sounds important to the content, including beeps from electronic or medical devices, phones ringing, doorbells, sounds made by tools or implements, and many others.

It may also contain unwanted noises, including overheard conversations, wind, traffic, talk among the crew, and other undesirable sounds. The task of the editor is to enhance the wanted sound and minimize or remove the unwanted. Here is where we run up against some of the limitations of the inexpensive editing programs, in that their sound editing is often not as sophisticated as their video editing.

FIGURE 18.1. *Marquee Select a Sound.*

Some editors, for example, have tools to improve sound by filtering out wind noise, pops, and sibilants (emphasized P or S sounds, for example) and to increase or decrease volume. These are very useful and can improve the sound noticeably.

Some programs can export the sound to a more capable sound editor, such as Adobe Soundbooth or the free Audacity sound tools. With these, it may be possible to remove the unwanted sound of an auto horn without removing other sounds. An auto horn typically has sounds at two frequencies (pitches). The horn sound may be visible on the waveform displayed in the sound editor (see Figure 18.1). Or you may be able to select the sound, play just the selected sound to confirm that it is the sound you want to delete, then reduce the volume of just that sound.

Note that we can't totally delete a sound. Normally, what we have to do is reduce the level or volume of the sound (or increase it—the tools will do either). A 3 decibel (dB) decrease cuts the sound by approximately half.

An auto horn is a well-defined sound (narrow frequency range, clear duration) and so is a relatively easy sound to identify and remove. An unwanted conversation will not be so easy and, in fact, it may be impossible to clean up if the desired sound is also human speech at the same time. The two sounds will be too intertwined to clean up just one and enhance the other.

Some things just have to be done right, in the camera, the first time.

OK, but what if we do have sound with some undesirable sounds that are not going to clean up well? Here's where re-recording voices can save the video.

A common practice in feature films, in which virtually all dialog is re-recorded, we probably don't want to try to re-record voice tracks that need to be synched, as in talent-on-camera speech. It can be done through a process called "looping," in which short video clips are played repeatedly while the talent speaks the part, trying to synchronize the sound. It's also the process used, by the way, when a singer sings the song for a non-singing star, or when languages are dubbed for different audiences. Looping is very time-consuming and hard to do right with amateur equipment. We can improve the sound with voice-over.

VOICE-OVER NARRATION

In instructional video, a lot of the spoken audio need not be synched, but can be voice-over, or the video can be edited so that the visual content focuses on the subject of the video (a task, concept, etc.) and the source of the voice, even if talent on camera, is not always seen speaking. This sort of script is easy to record separately, as part of the edit process.

Most editing software provides a tool to record new sound. The new sound will usually be on a separate track, so it can be mixed with the camera audio, when desired. Where we want the newly recorded audio only, take the volume on the camera audio track down as far as it will go, or delete it if you can.

Using a good microphone and a quiet location, record the script onto the appropriate track in the video editor. Normally, it is helpful for the talent recording the narration to be able to watch the video, as a help to getting the timing right. But if the video isn't in final form, or the talent can't watch the video and read the script at the same time, no problem. Just record the narration, leaving pauses between scenes. These pauses will allow the editor to separate chunks of audio and place them at the right points on the timeline.

Where there is no audio, do not leave the audio track empty. It will be too quiet. Record silence either before or after the narration, in the same location and with the same mic, to fill in the gaps between spoken segments.

SOUND EFFECTS

Sometimes it is desirable to add other sounds to the video, to help make it more dramatic or effective. Say you're shooting video of a cooking demonstration and there is a shot of a boiling pot of water. It may be difficult to record the boiling sound well, but a quick search on the web turns up several sound effect libraries that include excellent boiling water sounds. Checking to make sure the sound is free and allowed for your intended use, copy the sound onto another track in the right place to accompany the close-up of the boiling water.

There are millions of sound effects available on the web. If the exact sound is not available, use a good sound editing program to modify the sound by combining it with other sounds, changing the volume, selectively decreasing or increasing the volume of selected frequencies over a selected time, or other changes.

For one project, I needed a sound that was quite loud, not very long (fifteen to twenty seconds), with a supernaturally evil ambience. Working with a musician, we combined thunder and the sounds of a tree breaking apart in the wind, overlaying one with the other, repeating some sounds irregularly, trimming out a midrange of frequencies, and cutting the beginning where the thunder was just starting. The final sound starts out with a crackle and very suddenly becomes quite loud, with higher tones of the tree breaking apart. The resulting sound is on the CV4TT website as a sound file.

MUSIC

We can also add music to the video. Music sets a mood for the video, although we generally do not want music playing continuously through the video. Mayer's Coherence Principle (Mayer, 2009) tells us that extraneous sounds are distracting from the main content of the video. But used as an intro, to gain attention, and paired with the same music at the end, music can add to the production.

Most editing programs will let you add a music track from a CD or an MP3 file. Once the music is there, adjust the volume to have an introduction, then fade it out, and bring it back up at the end. And that long silence in the middle makes it easy to adjust the end segment so that the music "pays off," that is, comes to a musically satisfying end.

So easy. But not so easy. Most music on CDs or MP3s is copyrighted. We do not generally have the right to use the music in a video. As with sound effects, we can go on the web and search for royalty-free music or music that can be licensed for a specific use, such as our video. That's one solution, and since there is a huge selection of music on the web that can be licensed for free or inexpensively, it's a place to start.

We do have other options. For one film I produced many years ago, I recruited a student musician to compose and play music for the film. Since it was original, there was no problem with copyright. You may have friends who would make music for your video in the same way.

Your editing software may have a background music tool that composes music, on the fly, to match the length of the video. The software generally offers many choices of style, song, and version, depending on the length needed. The music repeats and strings phrases together to make it play the required time and then ends appropriately. It's not award-winning music, but it works well for the purpose. It's probably easier than recruiting musician friends to make music for you. The repeats are not a concern if you use only the opening and ending, as recommended.

Whatever the source of music you choose, it should fit the mood of the video. For most instructional videos, all that is needed is something light and cheery, since the purpose is just to capture the learner's attention at the beginning and signal the end. Some videos, such as ones demonstrating interpersonal skills or used as case studies, may have other needs, so editors will choose music accordingly.

WILD SOUND

Wild sound refers to sounds that are not associated with specific events and times on the video. A exterior scene in a big city will include car horns and traffic noises; an interior party scene will include non-specific sounds of conversation, and maybe the tinkle of glasses. These sounds may be recorded with the video, as a separate shot. Or they may be adapted from sounds available on the web. Either way, these wild, ambient sounds add to the production without taking a lot of effort.

◼ ◼ ◼

Incorporating enhanced sound into a video takes a little effort, whether it is music, cleaned-up sound from talent, or sound effects. But the payoff is big, contributing to the professionalism of the finished video. Next we move to other effects.

CHAPTER

19

EFFECTS

The simplest transition from one shot to the next is the cut. The transition from one shot to the next occurs instantly, from one frame to the next. It is unobtrusive and by far the most common way to move from one shot to another.

There are times when a cut doesn't work. I was given a tape that someone else had shot. We were creating short videos (one or two minutes) for the website introducing each professor. It included a long, well-thought-out discourse by a professor. It was basically one long shot. Great stuff, but not what I needed. And there was no B-roll. There was nothing to cut away to so I could not extract a tight couple of minutes from the longer talk without leaving jump cuts.

Remember that we don't usually want to simply cut from one frame to a nearly identical one with the same subject in the same perspective. There will be a slight jump from one frame to the next since the person's position will always be somewhat different in the next shot. I reviewed the video, about twenty minutes, to figure out what the key ideas were that would suit the purpose and log the locations. With no shortage of content to work from, it took a little while, but they were there. Little nuggets of pure gold that, edited together, would introduce the professor, not just his research interests and teaching, but his personality.

But I didn't want any jump cuts and had no B-roll. The solution I chose was to use quick dissolves between shots. The dissolves covered the jump cuts and allowed the conversation to move along without drawing much attention to themselves. Watch for the quick dissolves in videos of talks or even in teaching videos.

Some edgy videos actually benefit from jump cuts. If you want a cinema-verite or documentary look, or just want to set a faster pace, carefully used jump cuts may be OK. A few food shows, like "Diners, Drive-Ins, and Dives," use some jump cuts, particularly in the scenes quickly demonstrating how a cook in a diner makes some special dish. The intent is to show the fast pace needed in a diner kitchen. The editors use jump cuts sparingly, but deftly. In these videos, the jump cuts are not of the person but, for example, of a mixing bowl into which the chef is adding ingredients. The camera (on a tripod) is focused on the bowl, in a fairly tight shot. The ingredients go in, showing hands with a pitcher or small bowl, with jump cuts between ingredients. The result is a quick pace, with minimal pain to editing purists.

TRANSITIONS

All editors include dozens or even hundreds of transitions or effects. They range from simple dissolves and fades to wipes, checkerboards, rotating wipes, and many more.

Dissolves, also called "cross dissolves" or "cross fades," blend two shots, with the first shot fading away while the next one fades in on top of it. Fades go to or come out of black.

These effects always draw attention to themselves, in the same way that animated transitions in PowerPoint draw attention. For that reason, transition effects should be used where they are important and convey some feeling or information—and nowhere else.

For example, to show passage of time, as when demonstrating a process that involves some waiting time, a dissolve from one shot to the next works well. A fade or dissolve should take very little time, but it does require a second or so. You will have to allow time in both shots for the dissolve. What the viewer sees is one scene fading away while the second one fades in.

To show a longer time, fade to black and then fade back up on the next scene. You will also use a fade from black and fade to black at the beginning and end of your video for a more professional look.

You may judiciously use more intrusive transitions to indicate a significant change in storyline, location, or time. Wipes, both straight line and of various shapes, checkerboards, pinwheels, and other transition effects are available and can convey feelings or meanings. A video on transportation, using wheels as a theme, may benefit from occasional use of a circle wipe to transition from one mode of transportation to another, for example.

TITLES

Titles refer to use of text on the screen. The text may be static or crawl or scroll across the screen. In videos that are part of a larger multimedia production, such as a website, you may need no titles at all, preferring to include that information in the larger production. Typical editors allow titles in many different fonts, colors, and sizes, plus some effects such as drop shadows or outlines. In addition, you have a choice of placing the title over video or on separate frames inserted into the video.

In stand-alone videos, you'll want a title for the video, and perhaps credits for various people involved in the production, and perhaps acknowledgements for those who have been very helpful. (We probably don't want to go the route of feature films, in which everyone, from the producer to the caterer, gets a credit.) But it is worth noting that some contributors to your low budget production may be happy to get a credit, since you may not be paying anyone.

In videos designed for learning, there are other important uses of titles. If we're making a video to demonstrate a lab procedure for chemistry, labeling reagents or lab equipment will be helpful, particularly if the equipment is new to the students. For the reagents, it may work to create a large type label for the container, which is visible in a close-up. Or show the normal container with a title superimposed on the screen.

It may also be useful in the chemistry demo video (or even a cooking video) to list quantities on the screen, although they should also be on accompanying web pages or a lab manual, perhaps in printable form.

It may be tempting for the new video producer to use titles where they really aren't the best way to convey information. For example, in a video re-creating a historical scene, we may not want to use titles to identify the characters. It might be better to use the script itself. As characters greet each other by name or introduce characters to each other ("Mr. Jefferson, I'm sure you know Mr. Adams from Massachusetts?"), the viewer also gets to know the characters. And the use of the script and characters to introduce each other is far less disrupting to the dramatic experience than using titles on the screen. Similarly, we don't need to use titles to identify places. If a video is set in New York City, is it necessary to place a title on the screen? Why not use some stock video of the Manhattan skyline or Brooklyn Bridge to set the stage? If a location doesn't have such obvious visual identifiers, include a sign in an opening scene to identify the location, if location is important. The sign might be on an office door or outside a museum or some other normally occurring identifier.

CHAPTER

20

YOUR ASSIGNMENT 4

In this assignment, you will edit the video that you shot for your previous assignment. Then you will make a DVD of the finished video.

This assignment may be a team project, or you may choose to have individual editing assignments. As a team project, share the editing duties, breaking the video up in scenes for each person to edit. As an individual assignment, each person has a copy of the original video and edits it, producing a personalized version of the video.

Edit

Using the script (as produced), the shot list, and notes from the shooting day, review the video assets and decide what to use in the video. Assemble the selected shots into a rough cut, and then finish editing, refining pace, adding cut-ins and cut-aways, effects, and improving the audio.

Make a DVD

Make a DVD from the video. Test it both in a computer and in a DVD player.

SECTION

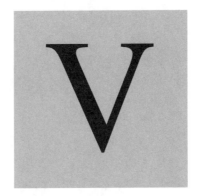

DISTRIBUTION AND USE

CHAPTER

21

VIDEO ON OPTICAL MEDIA

While distributing video on discs is far less common now than streaming video on the web, there may be times when you need to hand out discs. Maybe your learners do not have good Internet connections because they are in an unserved location, or an Internet connection is more expensive than they can reasonably afford. Perhaps because of confidentiality concerns you want to be able to retrieve copies of the video after use.

In this brief chapter we'll talk about different formats and capabilities of optical discs for video.

CD, DVD, BLU-RAY

First, let's look at the media choices we have. CDs, DVDs, and Blu-ray are all optical discs, in that the disc drive reads them with a laser. The laser light reflected back from the disc varies because of minute pits burned or pressed into the disc or other surface changes that affect how light is reflected. All of these are fully digital media.

If you have a high-def video clip and intend to play it on a computer, or you're just moving it from one computer to another, you can put it on a CD-R (a recordable CD), a DVD-R, or a writable Blu-ray (BD-R), depending on the size of the file.

The capacities vary. CD-Rs and CD-RW (rewritable) discs have a capacity of 700 MB or sometimes more, depending on the manufacturer. Most writable DVDs store 4.7 GB or 8.5 GB, although the higher capacity DVDs are not common.

Writable or rewritable Blu-ray discs are available up to 100 GB and more, truly huge capacity. As of this writing, relatively few computers have come up with drives that can write or rewrite Blu-ray discs.

To produce discs on your computer, you will normally use writable discs, CD-R, DVD-R, or BD-R. These allow you to record to a disc, one time. It's a good way to make discs for small-scale duplication. There are service companies that can make dozens or hundreds of copies from your disc at reasonable cost.

For thousands of discs, you'll want to go to a manufacturer, who will make a disc master that then allows thousands of discs to be stamped at lower cost per disc. The high cost of the master makes this production method workable only for large quantities.

Discs are also available as rewritable discs, CD-RW, DVD-RW, DVD+RW, DVD±RW, and BD-RE. These can be recorded, erased, and rerecorded many times. Because they cost more than one-time recordable discs, use these for backups and other repeated uses rather than distribution.

NOTE

The various symbols used with rewritable DVDs (-, +, ±) refer to slight variations in the technology. The disc should match the drive that you use to make the disc, although DVD±RW discs should be compatible with any drive.

In the discussion that follows, I associate particular discs with specific video formats. Note that the disc, as digital storage, does not limit you to one format. The video formats associated with CDs, DVDs, or Blu-ray are conventions of commercial production, as implemented in the players we can buy. That is, if you want to distribute discs to your family to view on their DVD or Blu-ray players, pay attention to the formats that are supported.

The next chapter includes a discussion of video formats, which are the same whether on the web or on disc.

VIDEO ON CD

While all of these discs are the same physical size (12 cm or about $4^3/_4$ inches in diameter), they do not hold the same amount of data.

The smallest are CDs, which hold about 650 MB. As audio storage, that's seventy-four minutes of music using the recording scheme common for commercial CDs.

Because video files are normally much larger than audio, we might expect that video CDs would hold much less video. And they do, if using similar compression. Since a minute of video, using settings intended to yield good-quality image and sound, might be 10 to 15 MB, a CD will not hold even an hour of video.

> ## NOTE
>
> Commercial video CDs (not sold much in the United States, but more common in Asia) will also hold about seventy-four minutes of video. The video CD uses a very compressed format, yielding about the same image quality as VHS tape.

The best use of CDs is to distribute smaller video files to students or colleagues. Many DVD players will not play video CDs, so they must be played on a computer.

DVDs

For longer videos, the DVD works well. It will hold feature-length movies plus additional content. We're not usually creating long videos, of course. But the DVD does have useful features that make it valuable for some instructional situations.

The DVD allows for a menu with chapters, and the player will bookmark the point at which the DVD is stopped so a student or instructor can restart a DVD at the same place if there is an interruption.

Commercial DVDs usually disable some user controls so the viewer cannot skip past the advertising or the copyright notice. We can allow full user control. That means we can present the viewer with a menu, perhaps of subtopics or episodes, and allow him or her to choose where to go next in the video. Used in a classroom, the instructor can play a chapter of the video and then facilitate a discussion, role play, or other activity based on the video.

BLU-RAY

The video on DVDs is standard definition. High definition video is normally delivered on Blu-ray, the highest capacity optical disc. It offers similar features to DVD except for the use of higher resolution video in a 9x16 aspect ratio. Menus, chapters, and bookmarks are also available, as on DVDs.

MAKING THE DISC

Some editors have built-in tools to make the disc. Pre-set values for compression and format simplify the production. If the editing software allows, it is helpful to create the disc image first and preview it, before actually burning the disc. This step makes it easy and less costly to catch errors in the disc process.

A disc image is a file that exactly replicates the contents of the DVD or CD. It will play on a computer just like a DVD or CD, except that you will double-click on the image file rather than place a physical disc in a drive.

If your editing software does not make discs, you can create the video files and use separate disc authoring software to make the image and burn the disc. Many disc authoring applications are available, some of which are free.

■ ■ ■

We have reviewed important features and capabilities of optical discs in this chapter. While most video is now distributed across the web, discs will continue to have a place in our distribution plans. They're also useful as a way to turn in video to an instructor, an option in one of the assignments.

CHAPTER

22

VIDEO ON THE WEB

The most common video delivery format for the last five years has been the World Wide Web. Sites such as Vimeo and YouTube, as well as single-purpose streaming sites such as Discovery Education, contain vast repositories of video from sources ranging from an individual with a smart phone to commercial cable TV channels. With all that video on the web, we might be tempted to think this is a mature and stable technology.

It is not.

Formats for video change and continue to change, for all sorts of reasons. (Most of the reasons do not have to do with technology, but let's take that discussion to a blog somewhere.)

The basic issue with video on the web is that video files are very large and Internet bandwidth is always limited, although the capacity continues to grow. In the days when most users had dial-up connections, video was limited to small images, slow frame rates (maybe eight frames per second or slower, rather than 30 fps standard video) and poor quality images, resulting from "lossy" compression and decompression.

Compression is necessary to make transporting video across the web as efficient as possible. It reduces file size at the cost of some loss of quality.

In this chapter we'll review features of various video formats, and then we can discuss how to embed video in a web page.

Early contenders for video include Apple QuickTime (.mov files), Real (rm), and Windows Media (.wmv), all of which required that the user install a plug-in or a player and some of which were not supported on all platforms (Windows, Mac, Linux, etc.). All of these still work, but are less common than they used to be. With declining use, the players are installed on fewer computers, further reducing demand for the format. (Windows Media player is an exception, as it comes installed on the huge base of Windows computers.)

NOTE

Readers with some technical knowledge will be aware that I am simplifying things in this discussion. My concern is to help video producers decide which formats to use on the web and not worry too much about what's happening inside containers such as MPEG or QuickTime. We'll essentially treat these as "black boxes." We know what they do without worrying overmuch about how they do it.

ADOBE FLASH

For several years, Adobe Flash video (.flv) was the standard. It was widely used on sites including YouTube and other large video sites and requires the Flash player, which at its peak claimed 97 percent penetration on desktops and laptops. One important advantage of Flash when it came into use was that it was easy to integrate video content directly into a web page, rather than requiring a separate player in another window, as had been common.

Such dominance also brought forth criticism of Flash, although its critics had long complained that Flash was slow and often used even when unnecessary, among other critiques. Flash video is a proprietary product, totally under the control of Adobe. Many users and producers prefer open standards, created by standards bodies, on the not unreasonable assumption that these open processes produce standards that do not benefit a single company.

The rising importance and market share of iOS devices, including Apple's iPhone, iPod, and iPad, dealt a serious blow to Flash, because those devices do not run Flash in any form. Flash is also said to run slowly on Android devices, another leading category of smart phones and tablets. It runs well only on a BlackBerry, the third group of smart phones.

MPEG AND MPEG-4

The ISO/IEC Moving Picture Expert Group developed the MPEG standards for video and audio. The standards have been issued with numeric suffixes, such as MPEG-1, -2 and -4. (The proposed MPEG-3 standard was merged into MPEG-2.) Each standard refers to a set of standards for encoding video and audio, along with other standards, such as the MPEG-4 intellectual property management and protection standard.

Because of strong industry support, MPEG in current and future versions will continue to be a useful standard. MPEG is recognized by ISO (International Standards Organization) and IEC (International Electrotechnical Commission), influential standard-setting bodies. The MPEG standards, in part, are also accepted by ITU (International Telecommunications Union), where they are called H.262 (MPEG-2 Video) and H.264 (MPEG-4 Advanced Video Coding).

Some parts of these standards are used separately. The popular MP3 audio standard used in many portable players is Audio Layer III of the MPEG-1 standard.

Each successive standard allows for higher-quality images. MPEG-1 was intended for use with compact discs, including the little-used video CD format. Compact discs (CDs) originally provided only 1.5 MBit per second data rates, sharply limiting the quality of video as well as the size of the image. The target quality was that of VHS videocassettes. By comparison, American HD broadcast TV has a data rate of a little over 19 MBit per second. Even at the relatively slow rate of MPEG-1, the computers of the day (1993) required added hardware in the form of a dedicated MPEG card to process the video images.

Digital video (cable and DVDs) takes advantage of the better quality of MPEG-2. This format allows full-screen, full-motion images at standard definition. Blu-ray discs use MPEG-4 to produce full-screen, full-motion video at high definition.

MPEG standards are subject to licensing, so that editors and players supporting MPEG are subject to royalty payments. Normally, these fees are included in the purchase price, though MPEG LA, the organization managing patents for MPEG, published a license fee schedule for Internet broadcasters, potentially including anyone who streams Internet video using MPEG-4. MPEG LA has announced that it will not charge royalties for Internet video that is free to end users, at least until 2015.

HTML5

All of the video formats we have talked about so far require a player of some kind. In some cases the player integrates well into a web page, as Flash video does. The need for a Flash player is essentially transparent to most end users, since the Flash player is so common. That there is a separate piece of software playing the video only becomes apparent when it is not there, as with Apple iOS devices.

Other players, such as QuickTime, are not as prevalent and the end user occasionally needs to download a player to view some content. This is usually not a problem, although it can be in a corporate or school setting where the normal end user does not have the administrator rights required to install new software.

As a way to avoid the need for a player of any kind, the World Wide Web Consortium (W3C) abandoned its own work on enhanced versions of HTML to adopt the independent work that was developing HTML5. This radically new version of HTML is intended to accommodate multimedia, including video, in the browser, rather than requiring an external player or browser plug-in.

At this writing (late 2011), some browsers support some HTML5 features. All support the <video> tag, but with different formats. Making things a little more complicated than we would like, formats have not settled out. It's a little like the format wars of the late 20th century, when Beta and VHS battled for market share in the videocassette business.

We've mentioned H.264 (MPEG-4) as a current standard. There are also Ogg Theora and WebM, open source formats not subject to royalty payments or concerns with potential patent infringement, as is H.264. Ogg Theora and WebM provide comparable performance to H.264 over the web.

These free and open source products are attractive to those who wish to avoid any potential royalties, such as the many users of other free and open source software, including the most common web server software.

As instructional developers, we usually do not know what browser, operating system, or plug-ins our learners have. In the corporate setting, such standards may be set by information technology, making things a little easier. But in the most usual case, we don't know.

The best workaround is to provide several formats. Additional formats don't require a great deal of work. When we're done editing, we render the video into some format or several formats. Some editing software refers to "produce" or "make movie" rather than the more technical "render." The software is assembling the final movie from the edits, effects, sounds, and other changes we've decided on while editing. When we want Flash video, for example, it is common to render to an .avi file, then use the Adobe Media Encoder or Flash Professional to make the .flv file. Many editors will directly produce an MPEG file. There are several video encoders for .ogg and WebM available, often for free.

If your editor will directly produce the formats you want, that's great. But likely it will not produce everything. In that case, we normally want to produce a format that is not very highly compressed, such as .avi, which we then convert to the target format. The converters available on the web will happily convert from any format to any other format. But the results may not make you happy. Highly compressed video, such as MPEG-4, usually does not convert well to other compressed formats.

Using HTML5, a <video> tag such as that shown below will let the browser play the format that it supports. The HTML5 video player will play the first version that works in the browser, making it easy to provide multiple formats without requiring the user to select one.

<video *other tags go here for controls, height and width*>

<source src="MyMovie.ogg" type="video/ogg" />

<source src="MyMovie.mp4" type="video/mp4" />

```
<source src="MyMovie.webm" type="video/webm" />
```

Your browser does not support the video tag.

```
</video>
```

This approach does not support Flash video, should you want to use it. At this time there is no simple approach to integrating Flash video into a page in a way that allows automatic selection at run-time of Flash or HTML5 native formats.

DEVELOPMENT: FINER POINTS

We talked through a development process earlier in Chapter 2, One Time Through the Process. We won't duplicate that discussion here. But you have learned a lot about video production between the time you read that chapter and reaching this one. Here we'll deal with some detail that might not have made sense earlier.

Use of Media

As you and your team design the final website, including video, some of your decisions do not have to do with content or instructional strategy as much as, Where do we put images or text that could as well be in video as on an HTML page? In practice, video producers want as much in video as possible and web developers want everything on the HTML page. That's not an approach that leads to rational decisions.

Let's dispose of the easy cases first. If your video needs a callout to label some apparatus, character, or location, include that in the video as a title. While we could overlay that on the player, it's not worth the trouble and we run the risk that it would not synchronize properly.

It's less obvious when the script calls for a question, display of a still image, or some other object that we want the learner to interact with. Perhaps we want the learner to respond to the question or study the image or manipulate an animation or simulation in some way. In these cases, it's usually better to display the content using HTML, rather than video. We'll probably get a better image using a still image compared to a freeze frame from the video. We will need HTML or JavaScript to process the learner's response to a question, so the stem of the question might as well be HTML.

The choice of HTML is even more compelling if the question content may vary, as might happen if the questions are drawn from a test item bank. Then HTML is clearly the medium of choice, rather than the static text on a video frame. With HTML we can set up a format that will display whatever question is fed to it by the test bank.

This last example suggests a guideline for deciding whether content should be in video or HTML: If it's likely to need to change, either for updates or for variable content, then use HTML. It is easier to update than video. For relatively static content, especially within a piece of video, put the images and text in the video.

Human Resources

Another consideration, of course, in deciding how much content is in video and how much in HTML is the resources available to your team for production. If video resources are scarce, then the decision tilts toward HTML. Similarly, if web development resources are thin, we'd lean to video. Note that this isn't a straight tradeoff. In general, creating web content is less labor-intensive than creating video. So if team resources are limited, more content will be HTML than video, reserving video for that content really impacted by video attributes, such as sound and motion, as well as the ability to transport the user somewhere else.

Fine-Tuning for the User's Environment

While we're developing the actual pages learners see and use, it's easy to become enthusiastic about the wonderful multimedia we're creating and forget what the learner's computing environment is. What works well with the fast computers and bandwidth of the development studio doesn't necessarily work as well out in the field. Up-front, we should have investigated the typical user's environment to look at screen size, browser, and connection speed. Although computer speed has become less important, as almost all recent computers are able to handle video, some schools use outdated equipment. Some locations have poor Internet connections, especially in developing countries or rural areas in the United States.

Early in the development process, test prototypes in the target environment. These prototypes should be sample modules, built using the same technology as will be in the final product. If performance or appearance is not acceptable, adjust image size, compression settings, or even the content, to make it work. It may be necessary to use less video and more images and text as a way to reduce bandwidth demands.

Video size is important because larger players demand larger files to get the same quality. When creating the Ogg, MP4, or Flash video files, there are settings that optimize image quality, sound quality, and file size. Experiment with different settings to see what works best for your target environment.

VIDEO OPTIONS

Using video within a website presents the developers with options about how the video looks and how it works.

When the page loads, before the video plays, we usually want to have an image in the player, depicting perhaps the first frame of the video, or another frame that tells the learner what this video is about. HTML5 provides a poster, that is, an image that serves as a placeholder before the video is available. In Flash, the developer can place an image in the player to serve the same purpose.

If the first frame is not particularly memorable or distinctive, consider an image of a main character, a medium shot of the setting, a graphic that relates to the video, or another image that communicates the feel or purpose of the video.

The developer may also choose to allow the video to play when the page loads, loop continuously, or provide controls (play, stop, rewind) for the learner to use. In general, we want to provide the learner with controls so that he or she decides when the video plays. That principle rules out playing as soon as the page loads and looping, that is, automatically repeating a video as soon as it reaches the end.

■ ■ ■

This chapter has reviewed the technologies available to us for placing video in a website, noting that the market is not yet stable. We anticipate changes away from Flash video, but the end environment is not yet clear. We also discussed some guidelines for deciding what content should be in video and what in HTML, noting some tradeoffs.

Whatever technology we use, we're reminded to use it keeping in mind the learner's technical environment so that what we create is useful and engaging.

CHAPTER

23

USING VIDEO IN YOUR TEACHING AND TRAINING

Once you've produced your video, let's use it effectively for teaching and learning. In this book we have sometimes talked about incorporating video into a website. And that's certainly a valuable use of video. But at least as often we'll want to use the video as a stand-alone piece, as part of a PowerPoint presentation, or otherwise incorporated into the classroom or other teaching environment. We can also use our new video production skills and confidence to assign our students to produce videos or use video as a tool to document events or to provide a mechanism for coaching performance.

This chapter addresses these uses of video.

STAND-ALONE VIDEO

I'm using the term "stand-alone video" to describe video that is not part of a website or a larger multimedia production. It is used as a learning object or content asset within a learning context, but does not itself contain everything we might include in an instructional or learning module. What might be omitted? It might not include an introduction or links to prior learning. It probably does not include practice questions or feedback.

What it probably does include is a demonstration, re-enactment, performance, or expert discussing a topic. It might include images and voice-overs to tell the story of an organization, school of thought, political event, or other more-or-less self-contained content.

Earlier in this book we used Merrill's First Principles as a way to look at learning. Recall that Merrill said that effective instruction should be problem-centered and include activation of prior learning, demonstration, practice, and integration into the learner's existing knowledge.

Stand-alone video pieces likely would not include all of these. But let's look at how a video might serve each of these needs. In each case, the instructor or instructional designer must provide the remaining elements to make the best use of the video asset.

PROBLEM-CENTERED

Instruction should focus on a real-world problem, which helps the learner apply the new knowledge and see the context in which the knowledge can be used.

Here are some ways to use video to set up a problem:

■ A chemistry lab assistant describes the experiment students need to perform in the lab, including a clear statement of what they are trying to find out.

■ An actor playing Isaac Newton talks about the challenge of calculating the position of a falling object as a way of showing the problems that calculus can help us solve.

■ A manager describes a performance issue that has arisen within his unit, as an introduction to a workshop on performance technology.

PRIOR KNOWLEDGE

Think of the video segment that introduces an episode in a continuing TV drama series. It may start with a phrase like, "Previously on 'The West Wing' . . ." and set up the characters and conflicts that will be important in this episode. Our video can summarize a previous activity, lab experiment, or demonstration, as a way of connecting prior knowledge to the new content of this class or module.

Perhaps it includes a brief summary by an actor playing an historical figure. Imagine one in which a student, playing Alexander Hamilton, summarizes Hamilton's economic positions. Use this as an intro to a discussion about early industrialization in the United States. Or, as an intro to a physics lab, a video reviews the basic physics of the phenomenon that is the subject of the lab. "Before we measure the acceleration due to gravity, let's look at an equation we've seen before, relating force, mass, and acceleration."

As an introduction to a workshop on diversity in a health care organization, a video by a human resources executive reminds participants of policies affecting respect between employees and patients for different cultures and belief systems.

DEMONSTRATION

Using video to demonstrate something is probably the most obvious and best use of video. By now you can probably provide your own examples, so I'll just list a few here:

■ Chemistry, biology, or physics lab exercises

■ A physical activity, such as hitting a baseball (use slow motion), swimming strokes, throwing a clay pot on a wheel, dissecting a frog, and many more

■ A process, such as dealing with a problem employee or student, writing a lab report, or critiquing a work of art

■ A procedure, such as calculating an average grade, replacing a component in a computer, or entering attendance data into a employee or student information system

Merrill's First Principles paper has further suggestions for us in how to use video for a demonstration. The demonstration needs to be consistent with the content. That means that, if we're demonstrating a concept, then the video must include examples of the concept and non-examples.

The first example should be an obvious, typical example. If the concept is "bird," then the first example should be a robin or wren, something the learners are familiar with. While a penguin is a bird, it is quite different from most other birds. We can use penguins for the demonstration after we have shown more typical birds and want to show some of the extremes. So penguins and ostriches come later. In each case we demonstrate how the examples have the characteristics of birds, such as being warm-blooded, having feathers, and laying eggs.

We also want to show non-examples. Bats share many characteristics of birds, but are not birds since they lack feathers and don't lay eggs. We will therefore want to show bats and explain why they are not birds, although they fly and are warm-blooded.

If we're demonstrating a procedure, then the video must show someone performing the procedure. It is not adequate merely to list the steps or describe the procedure. Show the procedure. Listing steps in the procedure can be helpful, but is not enough.

With procedures, also show when the procedure should be used and the range of situations in which it is applicable.

For rules and principles, show how they are used. For example, if we want to demonstrate the law of supply and demand, show how supply and demand affects prices. Scarcity drives prices up, as with gold. Abundance drives prices down, as with air. Also demonstrate the limitations of the rule: If prices go up, demand goes down, as long as the commodity is not a necessity or customers can substitute something else. Or prices may go up artificially because of monopoly pricing.

We can show those things by having an expert draw price/demand curves, or show illustrations of common items and discuss their prices, or through a dramatic scene in which actors talk about their shopping in terms of supply and demand: "As long as gas prices stay this high, I'm driving less."

PRACTICE AND FEEDBACK

While a video can't directly critique or coach a learner's performance, we can use video as an exemplar or checklist. Many of the videos described above can be used as an exemplar by pausing the action at key points to call out characteristics of a model performance or activity.

We can highlight or draw attention to specific features to be emulated or that a learner can check his or her own performance against in a number of ways:

- Text on the video can list important criteria.

- An outline drawn on the video image can show the desired shape or configuration.

- Slow motion can delineate a desired action or performance.

- A counter-example can show common errors: If your work shows this, correct it this way.

- For concepts, restate the required attributes and show how the instance includes or does not include them, depending on whether you're using an example or a non-example.

We may also use video to document learner performance or for critique by the instructor or by peers. Participants can use their smart phones, digital still cameras, or borrowed camcorders to record their speeches, presentations, musical or athletic performance, calculations, lab results, field trips, experiments, or other activities. Showing the video in class, studio, or in a conference with peers, facilitators, or faculty allows careful critiques, repetition for clarification, or study of still images.

These performance videos should probably not be edited, so the critiques are based on the actual performance, not selected moments.

INTEGRATION

In the integration step, we want the learner to make the new knowledge part of his or her repertoire of skills and knowledge. Video for integration may show the new skill or knowledge in a larger context: When would you use this skill? How does it relate to other things you have learned? Show the new knowledge or skill in a range of settings or contexts to promote transfer to real applications.

We can also assign students to create their own videos on the content of the instruction. It's a good alternative to written papers and allows for great creativity. Ask them to create videos explaining or giving examples of a principle or phenomenon. The construction of a video will help them integrate the new knowledge into their repertoire of skills and knowledge.

Beyond Merrill's First Principles, there are other uses of video in instruction or training.

VIDEO STORY BY AN EXPERT

Video is an excellent tool for recording experts or prominent people talking about their areas of expertise.

Ask an engineer or members of a design and development team to talk about a recent project, including the challenges they met and overcame or things they would do differently next time. Also talk about things that went well and how they intend to build on their success in future projects.

Many politicians host open meetings or coffee hours for constituents. By prior arrangement, students may be able to ask questions or discuss local issues for the camera. The discussions themselves are valuable learning experiences. The recordings become tools that can be used over and over to illustrate how people deal with important issues and what the different positions on issues might be.

Field trips are another opportunity to use video to make a record of the event. Again, by prior permission, it may be possible to shoot video of some trips. Concerts and plays generally forbid video recording, but the performers may make themselves available to talk about their art.

DOCUMENTATION

A final use of stand-alone video is to document important events in the life of a school, organization, or individual. New or remodeled facilities, graduations, beginnings of classes or seminars, and many other events call out for video to tell their stories to those who cannot be there or who come along later and want to know the stories.

VIDEO IN POWERPOINT OR SIMILAR PRODUCTS

You can, of course, add video to a presentation that you've created in Microsoft PowerPoint, Apple Keynote, OpenOffice Impress, or LibreOffice Impress. (The latter two are free and open source office productivity suites that, to a large extent, duplicate Microsoft Office, for free.)

> ## NOTE
>
> Free and open source software is not always no-cost, though the two I've mentioned here are. Open source software is created and maintained by a community of developers. It is licensed so that anyone can use it and distribute it, or even make changes to it, since the source code (programming) is always available to anyone.

It would be nice if inserting a video in a presentation were as simple as inserting an image, but it's not. The biggest problem is that none of the presentation programs embed the video in the presentation. They work that way because video files, as you know by now, tend to be very large. Because the video stays as a separate file, when you move your presentation from one computer to another or put it up on a learning management system, you have to take some precautions. The second problem is that not all video formats work. It is sometimes hard to predict what will work and what will not.

File Formats

Some format choices are easy. In PowerPoint on a Windows computer, the Windows media formats, such as .avi and .wmv, will always work. Similarly, with Keynote, QuickTime (.mov and .qt), Apple formats, will always work, as will MP4, a video format that includes QuickTime video.

Beyond that simple generality, things get a little trickier. On PowerPoint, if the computer has the Apple QuickTime player, any of the Apple formats and MP4 will play.

With the open source presentation packages, at this point it is better to try it and see what works. Many file types are listed in the Insert Movie dialog, but all do not work well. In one attempt, an MP4 file only played the sound and showed no video. An .mpg (MPEG-2) of the same video played just fine.

Moving to a Different Computer

You need to move both files, the presentation file and the video. If the presentation file, regardless of what program you used to create it, and video file were originally in the same folder, it may work as soon as you copy it to the new computer. Then again, it may not. If the video was from a different folder, it will not work. You must open the presentation file and relink the video.

Web Video

PowerPoint 2010 will allow a live link to any web video, so you do not have the video on your computer. It works as long as you have a fast, live Internet connection while you are presenting your class or talk. The process for versions prior to 2010 is a little techie, but not so much that you can't do it. There are several sites on the web that show or tell you how to do it. It's easiest with video from YouTube. I'm not including it here because there are a lot of variations depending on which version of PowerPoint you have and where the video is. Assuming the improvements in PowerPoint 2010 stay in future versions, it will only become easier.

At present (2011), as far as I can tell, inserting web video into Keynote or the open source programs is not possible. You must capture the video so you have the file on your computer, which may violate others' copyright.

NOTE

Why is linking not a copyright violation, but capturing it might be? When you link to a video, you are not making a permanent copy. You're just playing it from the web. If you capture it so you have the file on your computer, you are making a copy.

While we have assumed for most of this book that the videos we produce are part of a larger website or multimedia production, there are many other uses of video in education or training. This chapter has listed ideas, in the context of Merrill's First Principles, as well as other uses of video for learning.

REFERENCES

Aldrich, C. (2005). *Learning by doing: A comprehensive guide to simulations, computer games, and pedagogy in e-learning and other educational experiences*. San Francisco: Pfeiffer.

Clark, R.C. (2008). *Developing technical training: A structured approach for developing classroom and computer-based instructional materials* (3rd ed.). San Francisco: Pfeiffer.

Clark, R.C., & Mayer, R.E. (2008). *e-Learning and the science of instruction: Proven guidelines for consumers and designers of multimedia learning* (2nd ed.). San Francisco: Pfeiffer.

Clark, R.C., & Mayer, R.E. (2012). *e-Learning and the science of instruction: Proven guidelines for consumers and designers of multimedia learning* (3rd ed.). San Francisco: Pfeiffer.

Clark, R.C., Nguyen, F., & Sweller, J. (2006). *Efficiency in learning: Evidence-based guidelines to manage cognitive load*. San Francisco: Pfeiffer.

Gustafson, K.L., & Branch, R.M. (2007). What is instructional design? In R.A. Reiser & J.V. Dempsey. *Trends and issues in instructional design and technology* (2nd ed.). Upper Saddle River, NJ: Pearson Merrill Prentice-Hall.

Jonassen, D.H. (2004). *Learning to solve problems: An instructional design guide*. San Francisco: Pfeiffer.

Mayer, R.E. (2009). *Multimedia learning* (2nd ed.). New York: Cambridge University Press.

Merrill, M.D. (2002). First principles of instruction. *Educational Technology Research & Development*, *50*(3), 43–59.

SOURCES ON VIDEO PRODUCTION

Kindem, G., & Musberger, R.B. (2005). *Introduction to media production: The path to digital multimedia production*. Amsterdam: Elsevier/Focal Press

Millerson, G. (2001). *Video production handbook* (3rd ed.). Amsterdam: Elsevier/Focal Press.

Musberger, R.B. (2005). *Single-camera video production* (4th ed.). Amsterdam: Elsevier/Focal Press

Ward, P. (2000). *Digital video camerawork*. Oxford: Focal Press Media Manual.

ABOUT THE AUTHOR

Timothy W. Spannaus is program coordinator and senior lecturer in the Instructional Technology program at Wayne State University in Detroit. His teaching focus is interactive technologies, including multimedia, message design, and games and simulations. He is also director of the Certificate in University Teaching program. Prior to teaching at Wayne State, Tim was CEO of a multimedia learning consulting firm and held consulting, development, and management positions with several companies.

His research focuses on multimedia and scholarship of teaching and learning. He is a frequent presenter at scholarly conferences. He has held leadership positions in several associations, including serving as president of the Association for Development of Computer-Based Instructional Systems and the International Board of Standards for Training, Performance, and Instruction.

Tim earned his Ph.D. in instructional technology from Wayne State University after earning undergraduate and graduate degrees in radio-TV from the University of Illinois at Urbana-Champaign.

INDEX